# CHRIST REVEALED THROUGH *the* USE *of* SIMILTUDES

Acts of prophecy depicting Christ's salvation plan through the use of
Similitudes as stated in Hosea 12:10 (KJV) and other studies of importance.

## ROBERT SELIX
### THE PREACHER MAN

WESTBOW
PRESS®
A DIVISION OF THOMAS NELSON
& ZONDERVAN

WestBow Press books may be ordered through booksellers or by contacting:

WestBow Press
A Division of Thomas Nelson & Zondervan
1663 Liberty Drive
Bloomington, IN 47403
www.westbowpress.com
844-714-3454

Scripture quotations taken from The Holy Bible, New International Version® NIV® Copyright © 1973 1978 1984 2011 by Biblica, Inc. TM. Used by permission. All rights reserved worldwide.

Scripture taken from the King James Version of the Bible.

ISBN: 978-1-6642-1511-5 (sc)
ISBN: 978-1-6642-1512-2 (e)

Print information available on the last page.

WestBow Press rev. date: 12/03/2020

# CONTENTS

# DEDICATION

I would like to dedicate this book to Our Lord and Savior Jesus the Christ.
and the following

Chuck Missler @ Koinonia House
Coeur d'Alene ID

Chuck Smith @ Calvary Chapel
Costa Mesa, CA

The Writings of Arthur W Pink

All of which caused me to move in the Spirit on my journey of exploring the depths of God's Word as in Acts 17:11 and to my loving

Wife, Jaime Omera, that helped me put it all together to present to the body of Christ and all those interested in learning of the depths of God's Word.

# PREFACE

While in the mist of studying several diverse versions of The Holy Bible, my eyes fell upon Psalm 40:7 which stated: "And Lo I come, and the volume of the book is written of me." (KJV 1985) Zondervan Corp) I stopped in amazement at what I just read and pondered it...... Scanning in my mind, I recalled that I hadn't heard of the personage of Jesus being mentioned until the books of the New Testament. I spoke outloud and said "Lord we got a problem here, the volume of the book is not written of You. I have read through this book several times!"

To add more to the amazement, the Lord replied back. "You read it wrong." I instantly questioned the Lord by asking outloud, "How do you read something wrong?"

Upon that note, I realized it was late and it was time to go to sleep, this issue of reading it wrong consumed my thoughts as I fell asleep.

Upon waking the following morning, my mind jumped immediately upon searching out the answer to my question of "how could I have read it wrong?"

Diligent to search out the answer, I resumed to position of reading my bibles, just as I had the day before. When I searched where I left off reading last, I realized that the pages were not where I had left them, the pages were turned to Hosea; chapter 12:10 seemed to be raised and magnified in comparison to the other verses surrounding it. Hosea 12:10 read:

"I have also spoken by the prophets, and I have multiplied visions, and used similitudes, by the ministries of the prophets."

Stopping to understand what I just read, I focused upon the word - Similitudes, I didn't know what it meant. Upon this note, I realized that we had another problem!

Once again, speaking outloud, I asked "What is a similitude?" Searching in the books in front of me, I looked up the word similitude in the dictionary. Similitude means, the likeness of or the facts of commonality between two or more objects or subjects. (how are they similar?) Upon understanding this newly found theory, my mind focused in on Matthew 12:40 spoken by Jesus himself (in red letter edition) which stated:

"For as Jonah was three days and three nights in the belly of a huge fish, so shall the Son of Man be three days and three nights in the heart of the earth."

Here, upon reading this statement or similitude spoken of by Jesus himself, is where I began to understand its meaning.

I began to understand that Jonah was a similitude of Jesus, being in the belly of a great fish resembled Jesus in the tomb and the "vomiting" of Jonah upon the designated beach to fulfil his mission resembled Jesus resurrecting to his feet to carry out the rest of his mission.

I finally got it and upon that note, I started all the way back to the beginning of the bible (Genesis) to collect my findings of similitudes throughout the bible.

Though this is not an exhaustive version, I pray you will read through to see the Son of God in all scripture, in many different ways, but always pointing to Jesus life, crucifixion, resurrection and redemption for all mankind.

# ABRAHAM
# AND ISAAC

Please read and study the story of Abraham and his son Isaac to understand the similitudes pertaining to Christ, portrayed through Acts of faith and obedience.

Being on the same mount that Jesus was later crucified upon, we can see God's redemptive plan to save through these details envolved.

2 TIMOTHY 3:16
2 TIMOTHY 2:15
ACT'S 17:11
ROMANS 15:4
HOSEA 12:10

## G E N E S I S

GENESIS
CHAPTER 22:1-24

## :A B R A H A M   A N D   I S A A C:

Taught to us by the Holy Spirit by the use of similitudes. As a model or type of our Father in heaven, His beloved Son, our Saviour, and the Holy Spirit, our Counselor.

This chapter is beyond interesting for a number of reasons. One of them being, it involves one the most fascinating individuals in the book of Genesis. The man of faith, Abraham. At the climax of his life. We have seen his faith tested again and again in the chapters before the one in which we are about to study. Note please I said tested, not tempted. As the first verse states. (Note please Exodus 20:20 and Deuteronomy 8:2.) (This is also expounded on by the Holy Spirit)
(in the book of James, see chapter 1:12-15.)

God is not tempting Abraham, God is testing Abraham to see what is in his heart. And may I say, Abraham passed the test with flying colors. We are also going to glean from this study some lessons about the nature of the message of Him with which we have to deal. We are going to see just how far the Holy Spirit will go to convey to us His Truth.

But before we jump into Genesis I would like to propose a few interesting problems. Turn with me to 1-Corinthians chapter 15. If I was to ask you what is the Gospel? You might respond as such, (The Good News). And right you would be. But, if I was to ask you to define just what the essential kernal of the Gospel is. You might answer with one of many good responses, which would be right, in and of themselves. But one of the best responses to this question occurs in 1-Corinthians 15:3-4:

1. Christ died for our sins.
2. That He was buried.
3. That He raised on the third day, According to the Scriptures.

The question to be asked of us is, (ACCORDING TO WHAT SCRIPTURES?) Paul is not referring to the New Testament. Paul is referencing us back to the Old Testament.

To Prophecy. (See Luke 24:27 and verse 32. As one example). Remember please the New Testament was not written as of yet, or it was in the process of being written. But to know with a certainty that this is the essential kernal of the Gospel. This basic truth of Christ Jesus is that which is attacked by every cult in the world.

Now back to that passage of Scripture found in 1 Corinthians 15:3-4

- • That He died for our sins.== See, Isaiah 53:1-12
- • That He was buried.== See, Isaiah 53:8-9
- • That He raised on the third day== ?????????? Where does the Scripture state this fact "in the Old Testament? In plain print. (It does not). ??? is revealed in the Old Testament through (Similitudes, models, types) (metaphors, allegorys.)

I will use as my foundation in making such a statement GOD'S WORD. Please note Peter 1:20-21, = 2 Timothy 3:16-17 and Hosea 12:10. This will be our spring board into Genesis chapter 22:1-24. (Please look up the meaning of the word similitude yourself.

If I was to ask you where does it say in the Old Testament that Jesus would rise again on the third day?? Some of you might say "The book of Jonah", but that is cheating because Jesus told us so. Jesus Himself taught us in Matthew 12:40 and two other places in the New Testament relating to this issue by using a similitude. The fullfillment of Hosea 12:10 by our Saviour Himself. So as you can see we are on sound ground!!! Amen!!!!

In Isaiah 53:1-12, (Which is often referred to as the atonement chapter of the Old Testament) We see in plain print the prophecy concerning our Saviours death and the reason for His death. In verses 8 and 9 we are made aware of His burial. But there is no mention made of His resurrection. The resurrection is only taught by the Holy Spirit through models or types. This spiritual insight is hidden in similitudes. (See Proverbs 25:2 and Proverbs 2:1-6).

What I suggest to you, I submit to you, had you not had the benefit of insight you probably could of read Jonah a long time before you became sensitive to the fact that these passages of scripture were prophetic. Pointing to our Saviour's death and resurrection!!!!!!!!

Before we jump into Genesis chapter 22. I suggest for your own homework assignment Galatians 3; - Romans 4; - and Hebrews chapter 11; which might help unveil some of the things we are about to look into. We are about to gaze upon such spiritual insights that to the natural mind might become a stumbling block. But as believers we know, a stumbling block to some is the Rock of Salvation to others. Amen!!!!

I am going to suggest to you that we are about to look at one of the most profound similitudes, models, or types in the whole Old Testament. Concerning many interesting facts, especially the resurrection of Christ Jesus Himself.

With the benefit of the New Testament as a commentary relating to the Old Testament. We are able to look back into the book of Genesis chapter 2 with profound insight. Note please Galatians Chapter 3:6-8!! "The gospel was preached in advance to Abraham"

Abraham knew of the promised seed!! (See Galatians 3:16-19). And because of this fact given to us by the Holy Spirit in the book of Galatians. I believe Abraham knew he was acting out prophecy!! I will expound on this statement with scripture as we continue in our study together. Concerning the promised seed just mentioned see Genesis chapter 3:15. This promised seed was to carry on through Abraham by Isaac. (See Genesis 15:4-5, 17:4- note verses 15 and 16, but pay close attention to verse 19. The everlasting covenant spoken to Abraham was to carry on through Isaac. (Also reference Galatians 4:21-31, but note please v; 28 and 30.)!!!

Please consider this: When chapter 22 of Genesis begins Isaac is yet to have children. Abraham knew this fact. Abraham also knew of God's promise to him concerning Isaac and Isaac descendants!! (Amem)!! I am going to suggest to you because of these facts in the scriptures that Abraham believed God was going to raise Isaac from the dead. The day the commandment came, and Abraham walked in this faith. (See Hebrews 11:17-19). We are told by the Holy Spirit Himself that this is the rabbinical line of reasoning in the book of Hebrews chapter 11:

GENESIS CHAPTER 22:1-24:

22:1. "Some time later" (means after these things) After what things??

After 60 years of God refinning Abraham. The Holy Spirit is hinting to the fact that the things which are about to take place in this chapter wouldn't take place until the preparation was layed. That is to bring Abraham to this point in time in his faith. This will become obvious when we see what Abraham is told to do.

V:2. "Take your son, your <u>ONLY SON</u>, Isaac, whom you <u>LOVE</u>!!

Note please this is the first place love is mention in the Bible. Also note it makes mention of a son. Note the statement <u>ONLY SON</u>. The Holy Spirit is pointing ahead to another passage of scripture not yet written when this was recorded. (See John 3:16)!!! Where we see another Father offering up His Only Son whom He also loved as a burnt offering or sacrifice. Remember please the author of this book and all the books of the Bible is our Father in Heaven. And Abraham is placed in the role of Our Heavenly Father by type before we even get pass verse 2. Also note Isaac has already been placed by type, or model, IN the role of our Savior by the Holy Spirit in verse 2. Because he is the Only Son, Loved of the father which is to be the offering the sacrifice.

If you are an alert student of scripture you will take notice of another interesting statement in verse 2. "<u>Your Only Son</u>"

Isaac was not Abraham's only son. Ishmael was born before Isaac, 13 years before Isaac. (See Genesis 16:1-4 and verse 14. Ishmael means (God hears). Interesting is the fact that God does not use the son born of the flesh to fullfill His purpose here in Genesis 22. Which was to point ahead to the promise seed. Who we know to be Christ Jesus. God goes so far as to paint us a picture of His Son, to also have Isaac born by the means of a miraculous birth. (See Genesis 17:15-22, also Isaiah 7:14.).

As we continue in verse 2 we see that Abraham is told to go to a mountain in Moriah!! Turn with me to 2 Chronicles 3:1. The word Moriah is used there in reference to Jerusalem. Allow me to ask you a question. What city was our Saviour crucified in?? (Amem)!!!!!! On the very same mountain as in Genesis chapter 22. As we will see not only here, but as we continue in our study together in Genesis 22.

V:3. "Early the next morning"

The Holy Spirit draws our attention to the fact that Abraham rose early in response to God's command!! Drawing us back to the first words of verse 1. Emphasizing the growth in Abrahams walk with God, by his prompt obedience. And allowing us to see that we are on sound ground concerning our understanding of verse 1.

"Abraham took with him two servants."

???2 being the number of witness. (See Deuteronomy 19:15 and 17:7). In the New Testament in the book of Matthew 27:38, Luke 23:32, John 19:18. There were 2 men crucified along side our beloved Saviour. Remember please our approach to this chapter and the paralles we are looking for. Isaac was forshadowing that which was yet to come. Notice who is orchestrating this. In the spiritual sence our Father above. But in the here and now, Abraham was setting the stage. And who before the foundation of the world provided the unbleshed lamb, GOD!! (See Revelation 13:8 and 1 Peter 1:20.).

Turn with me to Genesis chapter 15. Looking at verses 2 and 3. We are given insight into something wonderful by the Holy Spirit concerning Abraham's eldest servant. Who's name is Eliezer. Which means (Comfortor)!! Whom we know to be the Holy Spirit. (Comforter== see John 14:16==King James version, ABS). Look now at John 16:13-14, speaking of the comforter as counselor, these passages make mention to the fact that he will not speak on His own, He will bring all glory unto me =(CHRIST). We have our view here in verse 3 an unnamed servant at the base of Mount Moriah. Who is there to bear witness. May I ask of you another question? Is not the comforter (Holy Spirit) at work in the hearts of some of the people at the foot of our Saviours Cross on the day in which He was crucified?? (Yes, Amen)!!! As I stated earlier God paints us a complete picture of what is to come. (See AMOS 3:7) As another bases for our foundation.

Remember God leaves nothing undone. He gives us an answer to all we may ask in the pages of the Bible. When you search for Him as you would a hidden treasure. (Proverbs 2:1-6). "It is the glory of God to conceal a thing. And it is the glory of kings to search a thing out" (Proverbs 25:2). When you rightly divide or correctly handle the Word of truth". (2 Timothy 2:15).

Our Heavenly Father has even gone so far to bring into our view the comfortor were in Genesis chapter 22:3. To teach us that the Holy Spirit would be and was at work in the hearts of God's children the day in which His beloved Son was offered up unto God as a sweet savor. As the comfortor is to this very day at work in the hearts of all those who are drawn to the cross of Christ Jesus Our Lord.

Before we move on pass verse 3, there is another point of interest which needs to be examined. "Abraham cut the wood". Abraham being the father of Isaac. And tyed by the Holy Spirit as our Heavenly Father. Who also provided the means in which His Son was to be sacrificed. (See Romans 8:32-- Romans 5:8-- John 3:16-- Colossians 1:22-- 2 Corinthians 5:17-21,--and Galatians 3:13, Just for starters.).

V4. "On the third (3rd) day Abraham looked up and saw the place in the distance".

First and foremost we are given the understanding that Abraham traveled three days. As did those who were with him. (INCLUDING ISAAC). Please allow me to ask another question of you. When did Abraham consider Isaac a lad??? The answer is, the day in which the commandment came. Abraham walked in his faith. And my authority for this is once again the Word of God. (See Hebrews 11:17-19). Now knowing this to be of a truth. On which day did Abraham receive Isaac back from the dead in the fullness of life?? (answer) <u>The third day</u>, when God provides a substitute offering in Verses 12-14. (Amem). (See Hebrews 11:17-19). As it was with <u>our precious Saviour</u>.

Nice how wonderfully God put this chapter together, For our learning. We might better understand who He is, And just what it is He has done for us. And we have just started into the verses of this chapter.

Seeing that I have lightly touched on verses 12-14. I will mention one more interesting fact concerning verse 13. The Ram that Abraham slew became an ordained offering in the Book of Leviticus. 9:2 & 1:10 and other verses.

Now concerning the things which we have just study. You might say that's ridiculous!!! But this is the rabbinical line of reasoning. And in fact Abraham knew it. Because he names the place that way in verse 14. But we will study that point of interest when we get there. This rabbinical line of reasoning is carried on into the New Testament by the Holy Spirit in the books of Romans chp 4, Galatians chp 3 and 4, and the book of Hebrews chp 11. As you might remember I commented on a homework assignment which you yourself needed to study in order that you might be able to see more clearly into these matters.

These notes are just a study aid to help you in your own study. As you begin to set your heart on things from above.

Continuing in verse 4.
V 4.
"Abraham look up and saw the place in the distance: This denotes a literal location, specifying a certain place geographically. As we will see more clearly as we continue in our study of these verses. But I am also reminded of what our Saviour said in the book of John 8:56. "Your father Abraham rejoiced at the thought of seeing my day <u>HE SAW IT AND WAS GLAD</u>." It is my personal belief that our Saviour is speaking of this chapter we are studying. Because Abraham knew he was acting out prophecy. As we will see in V:14. Note the wording in V:4, "<u>in the distance</u>". The more you study through the verses of scriptures throughout the whole Bible the more one becomes sensitive to the style of writing (finger prints) of the Holy Spirit. Remember there is one author to this collection of books, and one main theme. Always leading us to the Cross of our Kinsmam Redeemer, Christ Jesus our LORD. Stop here for a moment and open your heart to the Holy Spirit. And look at what is taking place in this chapter. Abraham was proceeding to do exactly what did take place on the very same mount some 2000 years later.--(coincidence)? I don't think so!! And once again I am reminded

of another statement but this time it came from a teacher I knew in the Word of God. "There are NO coincidences in the Kingdom of God, coincidence in the Kingdom is not a kosher!! word, (Amen)!!

V5.

"I and the Boy". Don't be fooled by the poor translation of the English. The Hebrew word is Lad. And translates== (armed soldier). And there is some evidence to the fact that Isaac was 33 years old when this was taking place. (See Genesis 21:34). As one reference. And I am not going to complete your study for you. If you desire more information, search a thing out. (Proverbs 25:2).

So we have a willing father and a only son. Possibly foreshadowing John 3:16.
"We will worship and then (WE) will come back to you." Here it is. The conformation we were looking for!!!!! The Holy Spirit allows us to see and understand Abraham's convictions concerning his belief in God's resurrection of Isaac. (see Hebrews 11:17-19). Also note, "We will come back to you" (When ????) When they completed their worship, That same day!!! (Question== what day was it???== It was the 3rd day of their journey. We as believers just so happen to know of someone else who rose again on the 3rd day. Note the fullfillment of 1 Corinthians 15:4--"that He raised again on the 3rd day ACCORDING TO THE SCRIPTURES.!!!!!!!!! Abraham not only believed that God was going to resurrect Isaac, but Abraham believed that God was going to do it that same day!!!! Also it had to be A Son that was to be sacrificed, because of the whole concept of a Kinsman Redeemer, (See Revelations 5:5 and the whole book of Ruth. To help your understanding of the Kinsman:

V:6. "Abraham took the wood and placed it on Isaac."

Notice who is carrying the wood for the sacrifice. (Isaac was). Please look at John 19:17 our Saviour also carried the wood for His sacrifice!! This is also another hint to the fact that Isaac was not a little child, nor was he just a young man. Because the wood required to burn a body would be of a considerable amount. Not to mention that the mount which they proceeded to go up is 777 meters above sea level. (Amen)!!!!!!!! Or somewhere around 2400 ft above sea level. Think about it, then look again at chapter 21:34.

"Abraham carried the fire and the Knife".
In your studies throughout the pages of the Bible you will come to know that (FIRE) speaks of God's judgement. And the word knife in the Hebrew tongue is (Sword)-- (See

Hebrews 4:12--the sword is referenced to the Word. Abraham is carrying the judgement and the Word. As was our heavenly father bringing the judgement upon His Son at the Cross.--(Isaiah 53:4-6 and verse 10) and fullfilling His written Word. Which was spoken before the foundation of the world--(JOHN 1:1).

"The <u>two</u> of them went on <u>together</u>"

The Hebrew reading of this verse is. And the two of them went <u>in agreement</u>. The word (agreement) used here in the Hebrew allows us to look further to this passage of scripture, then the english allows with its use of the word (together). For how can two walk together, if they not be in <u>agreement</u>?? And the word agreement implies there was a free choice of all on each persons part. And if this be so, which it appears to be.

This would imply that Isaac was older then we are led to believe by our basic or elementary Sunday school teaching. The Holy Spirit keeps droping hints to the fact that Isaac was a man. And as we see how wonderfully the similitudes in this chapter are unfolding concerning the roles in which these two man are placed by GOD. We are also led to believe by the constant hinting of the Holy Spirit that Isaac was a man of the age of 33. (Why??) 33 years old. Because that was the age of our Saviour when He layed His life down.--(See John 15:13 <u>"Greater love has no man than this, that (HE) LAY DOWN HIS LIFE FOR HIS FRIENDS"</u> WHICH ISAAC BY CHOICE WAS ABOUT DO TO. "No man takes my life from me, I lay it down on my own accord". Which Isaac also had to be a type of!!! (Amen)!!!! but let's move on!!!

V:7. Speaks for itself. The language in this verse is clear enough.

V:8.
Once again the English has not done this passage of scripture any justice. And that is sad, because most people who read the Bible know not to go back to the original tongue to search out the true meaning of such and important passage of scripture as this is. The English reads: "God Himself will provide the lamb." Sad is the fact that the wording in the English here only points to the natural provision which will take place in verse 13: And if you did not have the benefit of the New Testament, that would be your only understanding of this verse.

In the original tongue: "God will PROVIDE HIMSELF the lamb," as the burnt offering". The wording here has far greater implication then that of the English. It is stating to the fact that God will be the offering, Himself. As we know to be the case in the New

Testament. The wording here speaks not only of the natural provision, as the English did, but also of the Spiritual.

The last half of verse 8: "And the two of them went on <u>together</u>."

<u>agreement</u>."

This is the second time this word is used concerning their walk, relating to the issue at hand.

???. 2-Being the number of witness. The Holy Spirit is bearing witness to their oneness in heart. As was our Father in heaven and His Son, our Savior one in heart. (See Deuteronomy 19:15--17:6: John 10:30.)

V:9. "Abraham built an altar there and arranged the wood on it".

The Holy Spirit draws are attention to, – and by doing so allows us to see that the father provides the altar of sacrifice by which the son is to be offered up and presented unto God. As it was with our heavenly Father and His beloved Son, our Jesus. (Read Psalm 22:1-31, also note verse 28)

(Read Isaiah 53:1-12.)

As it is written: "Cursed is anyone who hangs upon a tree" Find it yourself. Notice the passage says, "Abraham arranged the wood". As God arranged all the circumstances which led to the atoning death of our beloved Saviour.

(Read Psalm 22:28 for starters)<br>(Read Isaiah 53:10)

"He bound his son Isaac and laid him on the altar:"

Of course Abraham had to bound the lad. But still all the same he did bind him. And I am reminded of our Saviour's prayer in the garden of Gethsemane.
"My Father, if it be possible, may this cup be taken from me. <u>Yet not my will, but as you will!!!!!</u> (Matthew 26:39) Question??-- was our Saviour's prayer unanswered?? Of course not, IT WAS THE FATHER'S WILL THAT HIS SON BE BRUISED FOR OUR INIQUITIES. (See Isaiah 53:10). (See Psalm 22:28)

Up to verse 9, and to the end of verse 9, we have been given a wonderfully perfect model, or type,-(similitude) of a foreshadowing of that which was yet to come some 2000 years later on the very same mount. God's provision for our sin. <u>A willing Father, an Only Son, who walked in agreement!!!</u>

ALL THAT WE HAVE JUST STUDY WAS TO REVEAL OUR HEAVENLY FATHER'S HEART TO GIVE TO US HIS ONLY SON WHO WAS IN AGREEMENT WITH THE FATHER-CONCERNING A <u>SUBSTITUTE</u> <u>OFFERING</u> FOR THE FORGIVENESS OF OUR SINS.

NOTE, THE WORD <u>SUBSTITUTE</u>. AND ON THAT NOTE WE WILL CONTINUE FROM VERSE 1, ONWARD.

Verse 11 onwards takes on a different flavor. As we see <u>God's intercession</u> and <u>provision</u> concerning the <u>substitude offering</u> <u>instead</u> of the Lad. I will also see how this relates to us. (Amen)!!!!!!!!!!!!!!!!!!!!!!!

V11. (<u>BUT</u>), We need to stop here for a brief moment and thank the Lord for such wonderful words as this one is. And when we see other words such as, (until), (if), (yet), (therefore), (most assuredly), (verily verily) and so on. Because these simple little words when spoken by God are bigger then the universe. And in many places of the Bible they are that which makes up our deliverance or not. As we see here in the very beginning of verse 11, and the intercession which is to follow in the provision of the <u>SUBSTITUTE OFFERING</u>!!!

V:11.

"But, the angel of the LORD called out from heaven, Abraham, Abraham!" This verse speakes on its own. The beginning of the intercession of the LORD.

V:12.

"Do not lay a hand on the lad," "Do not do anything to him. <u>Now I know that you fear God</u>," "(BECAUSE)"--here comes the answer-- YOU HAVE NOT WITHHELD FROM <u>ME</u> YOU SON, YOUR ONLY SON!!!

Here is the intercession. (Do not lay your hand upon the lad). And in this statement we are able to see the confirmation of the words spoken and written in verse 1. (Verse 1. "Some time later God <u>TESTED</u> Abraham"). We are able to see by that passage of scripture in verse one, and the verse in which we are now studying that God never intended for Abraham to slew the Lad. It was a test of Abraham's heart. Would he obey God no matter the cost?? And this brings us back to page one of our study together, where he made the statement that Abraham passed the test with flying colors. (Amen)!!

NOTE: In verse: 11. The <u>angel</u> of the <u>LORD</u> called out. (Who called out??) Now look at the last part of verse :12, which reads as such. "Because you have not withheld from

(ME). How interesting!! This angel of the LORD refers to Himself as God. Remember now what verse 1, says. That God Tested Abraham.

V:13.

Abraham loked up and there in a thicket he saw a ram caught by its horns, he went over took the ram and sacrificed it as a burnt offering INSTEAD of his son.!! (Question)--who provided the ram?? (Answer)--God did!!! The ram which was provided by God became the SUBSTITUTE OFFERING, INSTEAD of, or in the position of the lad. God is trying to teach us here that there needs to be a SUBSTITUTE OFFERING in our lives before we can be presented onto him as exceptable. This was also an object lesson and prophecy teaching us and leading us to our SUBSTITUTE OFFERING who was to become and is Christ Jesus our Lord. This substitute sacrifice, this provision was also taught and seen in one other place in the scripture before this in Genesis 3:21, where in the Garden of Eden God.. Himself once again provides for Adam and Eve by shedding innocence blood and cover's their shame by giving them coats of skin. Once again God provides the means of the sacrifice, the substitute offering, innocence blood!! We know it is sound doctrine because we see what God does in Genesis 3:21, and we watch the scene unfold in Genesis Chapter 4. ABLE brought a blood offering. How was it that ABLE knew to do this?? Because he was taught by his parents.
This substitute offering of a ram is later ordained in the book of Leviticus chapter 9:2. ==Exodus chp 29, ==Numbers chp 5, ==Genesis chp 15.

V:14.

So Abraham called the place "The LORD Will Provide," Or. "Jehovah Jireh" which means = The LORD our Provider.
Abraham names the place prophetically. Pointing ahead to the true substitute offering, which we know to be our Lord and Saviour Christ Jesus. This also allows us to see that Abraham knew he was acting out prophecy simply by the name he gives this place. And by the comment he makes in the remainder of the verse. (Note V;5--(8).
And on the MOUNTAIN OF THE LORD IT SHALL BE SEEN!!! (Question) what shall be seen?? (Answer= the provision of God, the substitute offering, the innocence blood to be shed. Instead of us, as it was with Isaac then!! So it was the very same mountain. (Amen)!!!!
GOD IS GOOD!!!!!!!!!!!!!!!!!!!!!!!!!!!!!!!!!!!!!!!!!!!!!!!!!!!!!!!!!!!!!!!!!!!!!

V:16.

Note please, the angel who speaking to Abraham swear's by Himself, declaring himself as LORD. As we saw by the wording in V:12. There are many such references as this in the Old Testament: (See Genesis 18:2-33-note V:10-14, 17, 20, and so on.

V:17.

Abraham receives blessings. And his descendants will be as numerous as the stars in the sky, and the sand on a sea shore. Note please, this is a two fold statement. (Stars in the sky,--as the redeemed!!). (and the sands of the sea shore, often speak of the Jew's) (See Daniel 12:2-4.) so note that there is another reference to Abraham's descendants in Genesis, a reference to his descendants being as the dust of the earth. Add them up./ There are three references concerning his descendants. Then study how Paul in the New Testament groups the people of this earth. He groups them into three categories, the Jews, the gentials who don't believe, and the (Redeemed, the Church).
??? so note, "all nations of the earth will be blessed because of you" and we see this passage of scripture fullfilled so well in the book of Ruth. When a Moabite by the name of Ruth is redeemed by Boaz, a jew. (See Jeremiah 13:1. Then read the book of Ruth!!!!!!!!!!!!!!!!!!

V:18.

"Because you have obeyed Me-(GOD)."
Note, once Abraham responded by faith in obedience to God's call, God reveals Himself and bestows the blessings. As it is in our lifes. God puts forth a call, waits for our response in faith meaning obedience, then reveals Himself and His purpose. It never works the other way!!

V:19

"Then Abraham returned to his servants, and they set off together!!!!!!!
<u>My question to you is where is Isaac????</u>

Reading through this Chapter, and these passages of scriptures relating to this chapter one naturally understands by the formation and the structure of the writings themselves that Isaac was not sacrificed. A substitude offering, a ram was placed in the position of the lad by God Himself. The lad was never offered up, so he never died. Henceforth we need to ask ourselves a question. Why has the Holy Spirit purposely edited out of the text the name of Isaac here in verse 19 of chapter 22??. Though we are given the general understanding by the Holy Spirit that Isaac did return with his father. So we are not misled by the context of the text themselves. (See verse 5 for example). (Plus the substitude offering itself in verse 13:).

<u>BUT THE QUESTION STILL REMAIN, WHERE IS ISAAC????? AND WHY IS HE EDITED OUT BY THE HOLY SPIRIT?????</u>

Through years of study one will become sensitive to the finger prints of the Holy Spirit upon each and every passage of scripture throughout the whole Bible. Sensitive to the fact that when there appears to be a contradiction in the scriptures such as this, the Holy Spirit is trying to teach us something. And it is worth one's time and effort in study to search this thing out. As Proverbs 25:2, tells us it will be. For at the end of your study there will be tears of great joy, and a heart full of love towards the Throne Room of Heaven. As the Holy Spirit reveal to you a truth which can't be found simply reading the Bible. (See footnotes on the top of the page).

Remember the reason for this study. We were approaching this study in the awareness of HOSEA 12:10. We were searching for similitudes, paralles, which in themselves would point ahead to our beloved Saviour Christ Jesus. And the fulfillment of 1 Corinthians 15:4, concerning our Saviour's resurrection and how it was spoken of in the Old Testament.

With these thoughts foremost in our minds, it is obvious why Isaac is not mentioned in verse 19. Remember Isaac was to be a type or model, a foreshadowing of our Saviour Christ Jesus. And our Saviour remained upon that Roman stake, <u>He did not come down</u>. Though He was enticed to do so by those who looked on, and though He had the power to do so, <u>HE DID NOT COME DOWN!!!</u> <u>HE REMAINED UPON THE MOUNT EVEN UNTO DEATH, EVEN UNTO THE</u> DEATH OF THE CROSS!!! (See Philipians 2:8).

Notice how wonderfully written this chapter truly is. The formation, the structuring of every word, the beauty that is able to be seen through the similitudes placed before us by the Holy Spirit for our learning, the fullfillment of Romans 15:4. He was laid in a rich man's tomb, (Isaiah 53:9).

So, as you can see, we are on sound ground concerning our approach to this chapter in its relation to Hosea 12:10. In the search of similitudes. Isaac is edited out of verse 19 because he was a model, a type of that which was yet to come in its fullness in Christ Jesus our Lord.

We need to become very sensitive to the subtleties in which the Holy Spirit writes and speaks to us through this most Holy text. Even in the nuances of a similitude. Because the Author of this book is God Himself, who is able to speak volumes in a single word, letter, within a similitude itself. (AMEN)!!!!

NOW WITH THIS UNDERSTANDING, LET'S LOOK AT SOMETHING WHICH IS BEYOND FASCINATING!!! A SIMILITUDE WHICH SPANS ALMOST 3 CHAPTERS.

Note please, Isaac has been edited out of verse 19 by the Holy Spirit for one reasons in which we just discussed. But, what I find fascinating is, not only here in verse 19 of chapter 22, but, he has also been edited out of the text for the next two and a half chapters. Where we see him at the well of Beer Lahai Roi, (meaning = <u>Well of Living Water</u>)!!!
<u>Making unto himself a Gential Bride</u>.!!!!! (GENESIS 24:62-66).

BEAUTIFULLY PERFECT, IS THIS MODEL, TYPE, FORESHADOWING, PROPHECY, WHICH SPEAKS VOLUMES CONCERNING OUR LORD'S SECOND COMING, IN FULLFILLMENT OF THESSALONIANS 4:15--18.<u>!!!!!</u>

In Genesis chapter 22, the Holy Spirit paints for us such a wonderful picture of what was still yet to come some 2000 years later, on the very same mount, concerning our substitute offering, a willing Son in agreement with His Father, taught through the use of similitudes.

<u>THE GOSPEL OF JESUS CHRIST OUR LORD, FORETOLD IN GENESIS 22:1-19, IN IT'S COMPLETE FULLNESS!!!!!!</u>
Study AMOS 3:7, "<u>Surely the Sovereign LORD does nothing without revealing His plan to His servants the prophets!!!!!</u>"

Note also how wonderfully the Holy Spirit not only lays forth the Gospel of Jesus Christ in Genesis Chapter 22 in its fullness. But, also by the editing of Isaac in the next 2 and a half chapters we have been given such a perfect model, such a precisely layed forth similitude (picture) of the ascension of our Savior, where He is absent from our view in the world. As Isaac is in the Holy text itself. (<u>UNTIL</u>) Isaac takes for himself a gentile bride who was <u>brought</u> to him by the <u>Comfortor</u> (Eliezer) by the well of Living Water. (<u>UNTIL</u>) the Lord is seen again in the clouds taking unto Himself a gentile bride (the church), to the WELL OF LIVING WATER!! 1 Thessalonians 4:15-18). (John 14:1-3 and <u>Isaiah 26:20</u>)

NOTE: The importance of what isn't said. Contrast this to what is said. And you will come to see that God speaks volumes in that which isn't said, as well as that which is spoken!!!

For example: Abraham, take your son, your <u>only</u> son??? Isaac. And note verse 19, compare this with the next two chapters, looking to 24:62-66.

WHAT A WONDERFULL CHAPTER, RICH WITH INSIGHTS, SPEAKING VOLUMES, TO THIS VERY DAY, ABOUT THE NATURE AND THE MESSAGE OF HIM WITH WHICH WE HAVE TO DEAL!!!!!!!!!!!!!!

Verses 20-24, speak for themselves. If you wish more insight, fullfill Acts 17:11, 2 Timothy 2:15, and Proverbs 25:2.

## GENESIS

### CHAPTER 24;1-66;

Read this chapter for yourself, for I am not going to give you a verse by verse breakdown. But, seeing that I have made mention of it, I felt it wouldn't be fair to leave you hanging. So I will help you by giving you a breakdown of the similitudes by listing them for your own study.

### :MODELS AND TYPES:
### SIMILITUDES

| Abraham: | As the Father: | ==== (F) |
|---|---|---|
| Isaac: | As the Son: | ==== (S) |
| Eliezer: | As the Holy Spirit: | ==== (HS) |
| Rebekah: | As the Bride, (Church): | ==== (B) |

1. (HS) is commissioned by the (F). (HS) is sent by the Father.
2. On behalf of the Son.
3. (HS) has full authority, meaning he rules over the household.
4. (HS) is instructed by the Father not to take a bride from among the cursed, (Canaanites), which was the curse prophesied about by Noah in Genesis 9:25.
5. (HS) is also instructed by the Father to take a bride from among His own people, the blood line of Shem. (cousin)
6. Just a little side note, earlier in Genesis 12:1 Abraham is called by the LORD to leave his home land. (See 11:31) Abraham is called out of the land of UR of the Chaldeans. He is called out of the land of what?? (Flame or fire, and Destruction), to go, and dwell in a land that I will show you. This land he was to, go to was Mesopotamia, which means the land (Between the Rivers).
7. Note, the bride is to brought to the Son.
8. Note the Father states, concerning the Son. Beware not to bring my bride there again!!! Question, what happens the second time Jesus comes back to earth?? He brings God's wrath, (See Revelation 19:11-16 and Zechariah 14:3-5).

9. The bride is to be gathered before the Son returns.
10. Note, the (HS) asked, what if the women is unwilling to come??
11. The Father's response, if the women is unwilling you (HS) are free of this oath, of mine!!
12. But, until then he (HS) is sworn to his mission.
13. The bride is to be gathered from Between the Rivers.
14. Ten camels, 10 being the number of completeness, (see Daniel 1:12 as one reference). What are the 10 camels carrying?? GIFTS. The camels are carrying gifts in there completeness. Abundance.
15. Note the gifts come from the Father.
16. But, the (HS) gives them as He see fit. 1 Corin 12:1-11 Note <u>V:11</u>
17. Note, the prayer in verse 12-15, is a prayer of intercession, by the (HS).
18. Note this takes place by a well, see John chapter 4. And Genesis 16:14.
19. Note also in His prayer, he will know that the women would be foreordained or (Predestined).
20. <u>BEFORE</u>, He had finished interceding, the bride came forth!!!! While he was in the mist of His ministry, the bride was called and came forth.
21. V;16, Very beautiful, a virgin: compare this to Ephesians 5:26-27 the whole book, 2 Corinthians 11:2.
22. Note the wording, "The <u>servant</u> <u>hurried</u> to <u>meet her</u>, And <u>asked</u> for a <u>drink</u>!!!" Note the women's reply, "<u>DRINK MY LORD</u>!!!!!" Now look at Matthew 25:34-46. (Interesting)!!!!!!!!
23. What's the first thing the (HS-Servant) does?? He gives her gifts. (See 1 Corinthians 12:1-11, note please verse (11), "Just as He determines".
24. Note V:27, speaking of His journey, "The LORD led me in the <u>WAY</u>!! Now look at the book of Acts, and see what the Christians walk was called, (WAY). Acts 9:2, 22:4, 19:9
25. V:34. This is the beginning of the intercession of the Holy Spirit Himself, read carefully. "<u>I</u> <u>am</u> the Fathers Servants."
26. V:36, The Father has given the son all that he has. (See Colossians 1:19).
27. V:45, Here is your authority, concerning the fact that you can pray in your heart.
28. (HS) gives gifts to the family too.
29. V:58, "So they called Rebekah and asked her, will you go with this man??" Note her response, "<u>I WILL GO</u>"
   A. This was a personal decision.
   B. To go with a man she never knew.
   C. To marry someone she has never met.
   D. To leave home never to return again.

E. Does this sound like the call that is set before each and every Believer?? Amen!!!!!

30. The Servant (HS) took the Bride. As the Holy Spirit leads us.

31. As they are on their journey back. Every night by the camp fire the servants tells Rebekah what it is going to be like with the bridegroom she has never met. All the while giving her gifts, telling her of her inheritance. Until one night, v:62. And the wedding takes place. At the well of Living water!!!! = Jer 2:13 = John 4:10, 14, Jer 17:13 so note, that the wedding didn't take place until Sarah had been removed. Sarah being a type of the nation Israel. "He came to that which was His own, but His own did not receive Him. Yet to all who did receive Him, to those He gave the right to become children of God. (John 1:11-12)" indeed there are those who are last who will be first, and the first who will be last!! (Luke 13:30 and Mark 10:31)"!!

So note, verse 67, And the Son was comforted, after the death of the Nations (Mother), how??? By the wedding of His bride!!!!

THE LORD BLESS YOU, AND KEEP YOU, MAY HE MAKE HIS FACE TO SHINE UPON YOU!!! BUT ISRAEL SHALL IN THE END DAYS FIND THE LORD ???25-26 ACTS ???

# JACOB AND ESAU

Here in these texts describe the lives and meanings of each brother born twins.

Esau, a man of the world

Jacob a quiet man with the promise of God on him.

At one point, turning enemies then reconciled later in life. Jacob, having a promise of God on him to make a great nation, God through great trials bondage all the way to the end.

Esau was departed in the opposite direction prior to the slavery issue after the reign of Joseph had passed. Please read on to see the similitudes that reside in this story.

2 Timothy 3:16
2 Timothy 2:15
Acts 17:11
Romans 15:4
Hosea 12:10
<u>Amos 3:7</u>

<u>G E N E S I S</u>

CHAPTER 25:19--
CHAPTER 27--

## :J A C O B   A N D   E S A U:

## <u>S E L L   O F   T H E   B I R T H   R I G H T</u>

<u>The Birth Right</u>, <u>The Right of the Firstborn:</u>

The firstborn is to receive a double portion, meaning share of all that his father has, (See Deuteronomy 21:15-17:). The firstborn would become the leader of said household, tribe or clan. And he would also become the Priest of said household.

The birth right could be forfeited, (if) certain things took place. As was the case with Esau. (See Genesis 25:29-34. As it was with Reuben, Jacob's firstborn, see Genesis 49:4. and 1 Chronicles 5:1).

## :J A C O B   A N D   E S A U:

The Holy Spirit seems to paint a picture right up front concerning these two, look to Genesis 25:21-23!!

1. Esau was a man of the field, what is the field typed as by our Saviour Himself in Matthew 13 through the parables?? The world. Esau is placed in the position of one being of the world!!! V:27
2. Jacob was a plain man, the word used here in the original tongue is tom, and means quiet Upright. V:27

The contrast continues:

3. Esau is typed as an unbeliever, as one of the world.
4. Jacob, surprizingly enough is a man of faith. (See Hebrews 11:21).

5. Esau was a hunter, therefore a stranger to peace. The only other hunter in the scripture is Nimrod. (See Genesis 10:8. Nimrod means the rebel.

6. Jacob is in contrast to this, staying among the tents, V:27. Therefore he is a pilgrim, (see Genesis 47:9 and Hebrews 11:13 - 16).

7. Interesting is what led to the sell of the birth right. Esau was not able to satisfy himself (the flesh) from the field (world).

8. Esau needed that which Jacob had. Which in and of itself is quite interesting. (Why)?? Because, if you are of the world or of the flesh; over all your thrist you will thrist again. As was the case with Esau, indeed he was of this vine. And he needed the one who had God's blessing, (see Genesis 25:23, 28:10-17) Interesting!!

9. Esau despised his birth right in the first place. What he is really saying to Jacob is, he can't live on promises. As it is with whomever is of the world.

10. The next mention of Esau is in the following chapter. Chapter 26:34. This is after the sell of the birth right. And the Holy Spirit makes mention to his age, which at this time he is 40 years of age. The Holy Spirit is hinting to the fact that Esau's probationary period is up. Note, that Esau has yet to repent. Study verse 34 and 35 carefully, and you will see that Esau married two women who were both Canaanites. They were not to be wed. See verse 35, these two girls were a source of grief to his parents.

11. We get the impression by the writings of the Holy Spirit that Esau is not in fellowship with God. Nor is he following the example of his father. Or counsel of his father. From a spiritual point of view Esau is in bad shape!!!!

12. What we do see in chapter 27 is. Isaac is still insensitive to God's will. (Why), because he still desires Esau over Jacob, because in verse 4 of chapter 27 Isaac wishes to bless Esau, Isaac has forgotten the prophecy of 25:23, which was given to Rebekah by the LORD.

13. Esau was guilty of bartering his devine privileges in exchange for his carnal gratification. Is there an Esau in all of us????!!!

14. Did Jacob earn the blessing??? (NO). Take comfort in this. Because Jacob is where you and I hope to be. We are like Esau, we are of the world. But what we really want to be is justified by faith as was Jacob. (See Hebrews 11:21.)

15. Jacob found the exceptance of his father, and received a blessing (Because), he sheltered himself or hid himself behind the name of the firstborn son. As we do in Christ Jesus our Lord.

16. Jacob was clothed in the firstborns son's garments.

## : JACOB TYPED AS THE NATION ISRAEL :

1. Jacob's name is changed to Israel, by God in Genesis Chapter 32:28.
2. Jacob is the object of God's election!! (See Genesis 25:23 and Romans 9:10-13).
3. Was the nation Israel?? (Yes) See Deuteronomy 6:1- and Amos 3:2.
4. Jacob was loved before he was borned. So was Israel the nation, (See Genesis 25:23 and Malachi 1:2, 3 and Romans 9:10-13. And Jeremiah 31:2, 3.
5. Jacob's name was changed to Israel, But is used according to his walk. When he is in the flesh, he is referred to as Jacob. But when he is walking in the spirit, he is referred to as Israel. This types the nation perfectly. As the nation walked, with or without God.
6. Jacob was to be served, See chapters 25:23 and 27:40. So is the Nation Israel during the millennium, See Isaiah 49:22-23.
7. Jacob is given an earthly inheritance. So is Israel, see Ezekiel 48:1-
8. Jacob valued the blessing of God. In fact he valued it so much he sought it in carnals ways. (Question, what was the problem with the Pharisees?? Was it, that they lacked a desire for the blessings of God?? No way!!! They tried to obtain it by carnal ways. Romans 10:1, 2-
9. And of course Jacob was exiled, because of his sin. As was the nation.
10. He spent his life as a wanderer... As did the nation!!!
11. He had no altar where he was exiled. As it is to this very day with the nation, see Hosea 3:4.
12. He yearned for his home land. As the nation did for almost 2000 thousand years.
13. He was dealt with unjustly while he was in exile. As it was with the Nation.
14. He was, and became a crafty schemer. Does that speak of the Jews or what??
15. He received a promise from God before he went into exile. (see 28:13-15.) As did the nation, read the Minor Prophets. Amos 9:15 (29:1)
16. But receives no further revelation while he is in exile until he is bidden to return to the land. Just like the nation.
17. He is preserved by Grace while in exile, As was the nation
18. He was the object of God's providence. Ezekiel 36:33-36.
19. Jacob does return, as God promised. And wealthy. As the nation has. Read, Romans chapter 9-chp-11.
20. Jacob comes back so wealthy he draws the enmity of those around him. But eventually becomes a blessing even to the gentiles. Read Romans 11:11, and 11:15!!!!!!!!!!!!!!!!!!! This types the nation so well!!!

THE REST I WILL LEAVE TO YOUR OWN STUDY!!! AMEN!!!

## : PUNISHMENT DUE :

HEBREWS 2:2;
<u>JOB 4:8</u>

1. EXODUS 1:22, = Exodus 14:28 where the waters covered Pharoh and the whole host of his army
2. Read Numbers chp 16; A fellow by the name of Korah, causes a cleff in the congregation of the Israelites. (How does he die)?? A cleff in the earth opens up, and swallows him alive. Interesting.
3. Judges 1:7.
4. 1Kings 21:18, - 22:38
5. Esther 7:9, 10 and 9:25.
6. Saul was there when Steven was stoned, (Acts 7:58, 59.) Now see Acts 14:19, Paul got stoned, but Barnabas got away, (see 14:14-20.) (Hebrews 2:2, possibly)!!!!

## : NOW, BACK TO JACOB :

21. Jacob went to some length to deceive his father.
22. As did Laban deceive Jacob, (with the firstborn also). And changed his wage 10 times.
23. BUT... Interesting is the fact that Jacob deceived his father by using the blood and the skins of a goat. And Jacob's sons deceive him by using the blood and the skins of a goat. (concerning Joseph). The fullfillment of Hebrews 2:2 and Job 4:8.
24. Also note: Jacob deceives Isaac concerning his favorite son.
25. As did Jacob's sons deceive him concerning his favorite son (Joseph).
26. Note, Esau hates Jacob. Esau is once again in the flesh.
27. Chapter 28:15: The promise given to Jacob by God (I WILL NEVER LEAVE YOU)!!! Is also given to Moses, Joshua, (Deut 31: and Joshua 1:58). Also given to Solomon when he built the temple. To the disciples before he left, as it is with us to this very day!!!!

By the way 34 of the laws of Moses were already in effect in the book of Genesis. Before Moses ever received them on the mount!!!

## : GOD'S LOVE FOREVER AND A DAY :

# JOSEPH

Here, in the story of Joseph are many similitudes to study and take a look at. It is a multifascated story with many meanings of God's redemptive plan to save all of Israel.

Going into Egypt during a time of famine with Joseph in charge and then 430 years (430) 8x12:40-42 later, leaving Egypt as a nation on their way to the promised land taking Joseph's bones along with them.

Here you will find fascinating similitudes and types relating to Jesus as Savior.

2 Timothy 3:16
2 Timothy 2:15
Acts 17:11
Romans 15:4
Hosea 12:10
Amos 3:7

GENESIS

Chapter 37, to 50:

: THE TYPOLOGY OF JOSEPH IN RELATION TO CHRIST JESUS :

While the New Testament nowhere authorizes the interpretation that Joseph is a type of Christ, the numerous factors of his life which point to this conclusion indicate in fact that Joseph is the most complete type of Christ in the Old Testament. As Joseph is a type of Christ in humiliation, so is he also in exaltation. Both were raised from humiliation to glory by the power of God. Even Pharaoh saw in Joseph one in whom was the Spirit of God (Gen. 41:38), and Christ is manifested in resurrection power as the very Son of God. Both during the time of exaltation but continued rejection by brethren take a Gentile bride and are blessing to Gentiles (Gen. 41:1-45; Acts 15:14; Rom. 11:11-12; Eph. 5:25-32). After the time of Gentile blessing begins to wane, both are received finally by their brethren and recognized as a savior and deliverer (Gen. 45:1-15; Rom. 11:1-27). Both exalt their brethren to places of honor and safety (Gen. 45:16-18; Isa. 65:17-25).

Joseph means "adder" or "God will add to me another son" (Gen. 30:24). Which God did for Rachel, (see chapter 35:16-18). Rachel named this child, "Ben-Oni", which means "son of my sorrow". But, his father changed his name to "Benjamin", meaning, "son of my right hand". Interesting is the fact that the scripture does not say that Jacob named the boy. Nor does the scripture say that Israel named the child. Scripture does say that his father changed the name of his son to "Son of My right Hand", meaning "Benjamin". The reason this is so provocative is because we (those in Christ) are also added "Joseph", to the father by the Son at His Right Hand. (Christ/Benjamin).

Both Joseph and Christ were born by special intervention of God (Gen. 30:22-24; Lk. 1:35). Both were objects of special love by their fathers (Gen. 37:3; Matt. 3:17; Jn. 3:35). Both were hated by their brethren (Gen. 37:4-8; Jn. 15:24-25). Both were rejected as rulers over their brethren (Gen. 37:8; Matt. 21:37-39; Jn. 15:24-25). Both were robbed of their robes (Gen. 37:23; Matt. 27:35). Both were conspired against and placed in the pitt of death (Gen. 37:18-24; Matt. 26:3-4; Matt. 27:35-37). Both were sold for silver (Gen. 37:28; Matt. 26:14-15; Matt. 27:3-8). Both became servants (Gen. 39:4; Phil. 2:7). Both were condemned through innocence (Gen. 39:8-20; Isa. 53:9; Matt. 27:19-24).

Joseph came looking for his brothers in Genesis 37:12 but they rejected him. Jesus, "came to that which was His own, but His own did not receive Him, John 1:11. Joseph was hated for his words spoken to his brothers (Gen. 37:8; Jn. 7:7, 8:40, 5:18, 6:41, 10:30-33.

Verse 7 of chapter 37, speak of Joseph's future sovereignty or reign over his brothers. Joseph, of coarse, knew this as did Jesus, (Matt. 26:64). Note verse 2 of chapter 37 in Genesis, Joseph is pictured as a shepherd. As was our Saviour, "The good Shepherd" John 10:11. Joseph, in time will shepherd over the whole know world of his day, (see chapter 41:39-40). So will our Jesus, see Daniel 2:34-35, 44-45.

Daniel chapter 7:21-27; Zech. 14:9; There are many more such verses. Note Vrs. 2, we are given insight by the Holy Spirit to the fact that Joseph despises evil, this fact is confirmed in chapter 39:9. We are, however, given insight, in Vrs. 2 of chapter 37, into this very issue by Joseph's action. He returns to his father giving him a bad report concerning his brothers. Note that the scripture does not say that Joseph gave Jacob a bad report, nor does it say Israel, it states, rather, the Father. (I hope and pray that you will become very sensitive to the style or "finger prints", meaning the structure by which the Holy Spirit writes and lays forth "similitudes".

Chapter 37:12-13. Note that Joseph is sent by Israel to speak to his brothers. This is what I just prayed about.
Sent by Israel!!!!!

## ISRAEL / GOVERNED BY GOD
### (Joseph was being led by God)

Joseph was being led by God to seek out his brothers; and whom was our beloved Savior sent by? (Is. 48:16; Jn. 3:16 FOR GOD SO LOVED THE WORLD THAT HE "GAVE HIS ONLY BEGOTTEN SON". As the Father here in this passage was sending His Son whom he loved to seek out His brethren, we now enter into a similitude. Which was in and of itself, a prophecy pointing ahead to the work of our Father through His Son, whom He loved. (Gen. 37:3, 12 & 13 then Jn. 3:16; 16:5 and 1:11; 1:14. Please note verse 14, "Go and see if all is well with your brothers and with the flocks" (Jn. 10:16; Isa 56:8; 48:6; 9:1&2; Jn. 1:12-13) and bring WORD back to me. (Acts 1:9 The Ascension.)

Valley of Hebron, meaning "fellowship or communion".
Vrs. 15, Joseph was in a field looking for his brothers. By Christ Himself the field is typed as the world, (See the parables, starting in Matt. 13:24). So Joseph was in the

world looking for his brothers. As was our Savior walking through the world looking for his brothers. (Jn. 1:11-14).

Vrs. 16, Joseph finds his brothers in Dothan. <u>Which means Law</u>, as in custom or tradition. Interesting, Jesus also found His brothers bound in the Law (Mk. 7:8) through their own customs, meaning "traditions".

Vrs. 18, They plotted to kill Him. (Matt. 12:14).

Vrs. 19 & 20, Joseph's brothers were in disbelief as was the Jewish nation as a whole (Rom. 11:25 & 26. Joseph is thrown into a waterless pit (Gen. 37:24). Jesus descends into the heart (or "bowels") of the earth. (Matt. 12:40 and 1 Pet. 3:19, 4:6).

Possibly, please note the word "possibly". Possibly, the Holy Spirit is hinting to the fact that Joseph was in the pit three days. Note Vrs. 29; "When Reuban returned". "Question"? How long was Reuban actually gone? Now please take your Bibles and turn with me to Chapter 42:17. Now my question to you is why did Joseph place his brothers in prison for three days. Possibly, that's how long they had him in a pit. Amen. Now turn with to Zech. 9:9 and read on to verse 11. Where the scripture once again makes mention to a waterless pit. Note the content of this passages, very interesting!! Look at Luke 16:19-31. I Pet. 3:18-20.

Vrs. 23, All of this is possibly laying forth a similitude in relation to the resurrection of Christ.

Vrs. 25, His brothers sat down, See Matt. 27:36.

Vrs. 26, Judah is the one who was desiring to sell his brother. Amen!!! But, what many don't know, is when translating the name Judah from the original text to the Greek in the New Testament, Judah is actually Judas! And who sold and betrayed our Savior? <u>Judas</u> (Matt. 26:14-16; 27: 3-8).

Both Jesus and Joseph were betrayed and sold, both for silver.
Reuben tore his clothes, as sighn of mourning. And Judas hung himself (Matt. 27:5).

Please read 37:31, 32 carefully. Joseph's brothers slaughtered a goat, dip the coat of Joseph in the blood, and presented it to his Father Jacob. Deceiving Jacob concerning his son whom he loved. As did Jacob, he slatered a goat and deceived Isaac, his father concerning the son whom Isaac loved. (Gen. 27:1-30). (Possibly Heb. 2:2 and Job 4:8; Rev. 3:19).

Question: In both cases mention above, to whom was the substituded blood presented to? (Answer, the father)!! As with our beloved Savior Himself. (Heb. 9:12-14: As the scapegoat of Leviticus 16:5-10)!! Also, the sustitude offering of Gen. 22:13.

Note V:33 Israel believed the lie. As did and still does the nation Israel concerning their Christ, (Romans 11:23).
V:36, Joseph is sold into Egypt. Joseph is sold into the world, we are bought for a price, by the shed blood of our Savior (Matt 26:14-16; 27:3-8, 1 Corin 6:20, and Acts 20:28). By our Savior being sold to the world by Judas!!!!

Chap. 39:---50:

V:2, The Lord was with Joseph, and Joseph prospered. See Isaiah 53:10; Jn. 15:5-7.
V:3, Joseph's master, who was a Gentile, saw that the Lord was with Joseph as He was with Daniel 2:46-49. As it is with us (Matt. 28:20b). We are Gentiles and we also know and understand that the LORD was with our Lord, and we also are aware of the fact that our Lord is the LORD thy GOD, as King Nebuchadnezzar was also aware of (Dan. 4:1-37).
V:4, Joseph found grace in his master's eyes (see Jn. 1:14 and V:17 and Philippians 2:9-11).

V:5, Joseph was in charge of all his master owned" (see Col. 1:12-20).
The Lord blessed everything because of Joseph. As are we blessed with all spiritual blessings in the heavenlies. (Eph. 2:4-10).

V: 7 and 8, Joseph was surely tested and tempted but he refused and stood against the temptation (Gen. 39:7-9). Also, see Lk. 4:1-13. Note: Joseph knew the sin would be against God and God alone. Note v:13-19: Joseph was accused falsely!! (see Is. 53:9 and Jn. 18:18). Joseph gave no defence (Is. 53:7) In Chapter 37:4 Joseph's brothers hated him because of envy (see Matt. 27:18).

Chapter 37, to 50:

## THE TYPOLOGY OF JOSEPH IN RELATION TO CHRIST JESUS

Joseph was cast into prison without a just verdict, (John 18:38; 19:6-b; Isa. 53:9; Ps. 35:11-12).
V:20, Joseph was put into prison!! As our Lord laid in a rich man's tomb, (Isa. 53:9).
V:21 But the Lord was with Joseph. As with our Lord. (Acts- 2:24-28, note 1 Peter 3:19). Also, note Joseph had all authority even when he was bond!! (Acts 2:23-28 and I Peter 3:18, -20 & 4:6).

Chapter 40:1-

## THE CUPBEARER, THE BAKER, AND JOSEPH

Note, The bread and wine are instituted here as a type in relation to Joseph as a type of Christ Jesus our Lord. This is also seen in Genesis Chapter 14:18, where we see Melchizedek, king of Salem, who was the Priest of the God Most High, blessing Abraham. (Question, was this Melchizedek a king and priest of the Gentiles? Also, was he a gentile himself? YES? (See rev. 1:6 and 5:10, where you will see that we are made to be Kings and priest unto our Lord, that we might reign with Him on earth (IPet. 2:5, 9).

V: 1-4; Joseph was numbered with two transgressors, though he was falsely accused. Such was the case with our Lord, (Matt. 24:7--Luke 23:41; Jn. 19:18.: In verse 8, Joseph placed himself in the position of a high priest, asking of the men their dreams desiring to intercede for them (Ezekiel 22:30-31, Genesis 18:22-33). Wonderful is the fact that we have a High Priest sitting at the right hand of God interceding for us night and day (see Romans 8:34 and Hebrews 7:25). Joseph interprets both mens dreams!! The bread (baker) is broken and hung upon a tree, (Genesis 40:19-22, Luke 22:19 and 23:33). The wine bearer is restored to the right hand of the king (V:21 Acts 1:9, 2:33, 36, 7:55). This is a perfect similitude of the Lord's last supper and resurrection in relation to His ascension. Note please; Joseph blessed the one man and cursed the other. (See Luke 23:43). The means of the blessing involved the one who handled the cup, (Blood Luke 22:20)!!!! If you look closely, this is where the Passover is first (Typed or instituted) by the Holy Spirit (Luke 22:13). Verse 8b, Joseph believed the dreams were of God and also knew this knowledge belonged to God. Understanding this fact he moved to intercede believing God was going to give understanding. As Jesus was well aware of all things (John 2:24, 25 11:11, 14 and 4:16-18). Verse 14, Joseph desired to be remembered, now look at Luke 22:19. All that Joseph said came true, sound like anyone we know??

A little side note: Both Joseph and Daniel rose to power by God giving them both interpretation to dreams (Daniel 2:1- And Genesis 40:1- and 41:1).

## CHAPTER 41:

Two full years have passed, the number (#2) being the number of witness (Deuteronomy 19:15, 17:6-7, and Matt 18:16). This is mention to bear witness to the chapter before this one in all its fullness, as we have just studied it in model or type. Also to let us know how long Joseph was bound, and of Joseph himself.

V:2, The number #7 is mentioned. Seven being the number of perfection, or completeness, or the attributes of God (Isaiah 11:2-4, Rev 1:20, 5:6). Note please verse 5 of chapter 41, where a second dream is given. This is confirmation by God, confirming the first dream, (see v:32). Which confirms Deuteronomy 19:15 and my first statement in this chapter. In verse 12, in reference to Joseph the word (Hebrew) is used. The word Hebrew means, (one who has crossed over) note, Genesis 14:13 where we first see it used of Abraham. Verse 16, Joseph understood and admitted he was unable to give the interpretation. He also understood and believed that God was able and would give the insight needed. Joseph gave all the glory to God.

Note: The man who was of the world, needed the man who was of God, to understand God's will. As it is with us and our Savior. As it is with the world to this very day, they need God's Son (Pray the Lord of the harvest to send workers into the harvest field).

V:25, God revealed, God gave the understanding (Amos 3:7, 4:13 Daniel 2:28-49, Isaiah 42:9). V:25-32, Joseph revelation to Pharaoh was followed by a season of plenty. Then a season of famine. As it is with the Nation Israel to this very day. The Nation Israel was blessed as Christ walked among them. But, a famine for the Word of God has fallen upon them (Amos 8:11). I believe this is a reference to the end times also (pray about this).

V:33, Joseph counsels Pharaoh, and continues to do so through the next 8 chapters. Joseph's role before Pharaoh is as a Wonderful Counselor (Isaiah 9:6-7). V:25-32, Joseph warns of the coming danger (Matt 24, Mk 13, Lk 21, Rev 6-chapter 19). Joseph spoke of provisions, as did our Savior (John 4:10, 6:27, and many more such verses).
Please note: The end of V;37, spoken by a gentile king, it is seen and understood that the Spirit of the God Most High is In Joseph. (Also see Daniel 2:46). Of Joseph it is first mentioned concerning the indwelling of the Spirit of God. Note the design by which the Holy Spirit first makes reference to a indwelling, and upon whom it is mentioned. Confirmation by the Holy Spirit that we should look to Joseph as a model of the original, the pre-incarnat Christ, the incarnation of His Word; Immanuel-God is with us; 1 John 1:1-4.

Romans 15:4; "For everything that was written before hand (in the past) was written to teach us, so that through the endurance and the encouragement of the Scripture we might have hope.

V:39-40: Joseph was given authority over all things, (Colossians 1:12-20). V:42, Joseph was given fine linen to wear (Revelation 19:7-8; 3:4-5; 3:18; 4:4; 6:11; 7:9; 19:14; Ezekiel 44:17-19; Zechariah 3:1-4;

V:43; Joseph's authority was publicly attested to. And they shouted bow the knee (Original tongue). As it is and shall be with our Savior. (John 11:32; 12:3; Philippians 2:9-11; Isaiah 45:22-24).

CHAPTER 41:

In verse 45: <u>Joseph is given a new name</u>. Please read Revelation 3:12; Jeremiah 23:5-6; 33:15-16; At the same time in verse 45, <u>Joseph is also given a gentile bride</u>. The Holy Spirit has placed before us in this study of Joseph one beautiful foreshadowing, similitude, of our Savior.

V:46; <u>JOSEPH WAS 30 YEARS OLD WHEN HE ENTERED HIS SERVICE TO PHARAOH. TURN TO LUKE 3:23!!!</u>

V:45; Joseph's new name has a double meaning, because it is given to him in two parts:

1.  Revealer of secrets!!!
2.  Savior of the world!!!

Please see Matthew 13:35 and Luke 19:10 and John 3:16-17.

V:50; Joseph fathered two son's. 1. Manasseh (forgetting) 2. Ephraim (faithfullness) And these two boys types the nation Israel's walk with God.
V:55; "Go to Joseph and do what he tells you" (Mark 9:7).

Now V:46-57:

1.  We see Joseph feeding the whole known world, (John 3:16; 6:25-35).
2.  He alone could give the bread of life, (John 6:27).
3.  He was a Savior to all peoples, (Isaiah 49:6, John 10:16).
4.  He did nothing for those who did not come to him, (John 3:18-21).
5.  The people had to act upon the blessing, (John 1:12-13).
6.  Interesting, the scripture states, there was more then enough grain (blessing) to meet the need of the world, (John 6:5-13).

CHAPTER 42:

Here we see Joseph's brothers in need of food. They must journey to a far land to purchase that which they need. Let's take a seek peek ahead to chapter 45:5-8. Here we see Joseph knew all this was done by the hand of God. The reason, to preserve a remnant (Romans 11:1-32).

GOD BROUGHT THE FAMINE: Pharaoh's dream in chapter 41: confirms this statement. As Joseph makes clear to us in 41:32. This was all done by God to fulfill His Words spoken to Abraham back in Genesis 15:12-16. That a nation would be born of the 12 sons of Jacob. But Jacob and his other 11 sons had to be moved to Egypt. So God move them, by the means of a famine.. We see this same type of thing take place once again when God desired to fulfill His Word in relation to Micah 5:2. God placed upon Caesar Augustus heart to take a census of the entire Roman world, to accomplish one goal, to move His Son, and His parents to Bethlehem in fulfillment of Micah 5:2, (see Luke 2:1-4). Know and understand this, the LORD THY GOD IS GOD, AND HE IS MORE THEN ABLE!!!!!.

V:6;    Joseph's brothers bow down to him (Genesis 37:7-8; 42:6b; Philippians 2:10-11; where we see there is a day coming when the whole universe will bow to our beloved Savior. (note Isaiah 45:22-24). V:8; Joseph recognized his brothers. But they did not recognized him, (John 1:10-11; and 7:5).

Chapter 42:

V:10: Note, Joseph's brothers call him lord. And refer to themselves as his servants. As we are to see ourselves in Christ Jesus our Lord. (Luke 17:10). V:17, Joseph puts his brothers in custody 3 days, which I have already expounded upon (Genesis 37:24).

V:18-20, Joseph tells them what they must do to live (John 10:11, 6:29, 37, 39-40).

In verse 21 Joseph's brothers admit their guilt. Please take your Bibles and turn with me to the book of Hosea, (if for no other reason then to loosen those pages of the Bible which we as believers seldom turn to). In Hosea 5:15 we find something quite interesting.

"THEN I WILL GO BACK TO MY PLACE UNTIL THEY ADMIT THEIR GUILT."
"AND THEY WILL SEEK MY FACE"
"IN THEIR MISERY THEY WILL EARNESTLY SEEK ME"
(Jeremiah 30:7=Matt 24:15.

In verse 18: Joseph is the first to speak of God.
In verse 24: Joseph wept!!! Jesus wept!!! (John 11:35)
Count the number of times Joseph wept (7) the number of completeness. (money faileth here)
V:25, Joseph gives them grain (the bread of life) but does not take their money. (Why)? Because the gift of God can not be bought (Acts 8:20, Revelation 21:6=Isaiah 55:1).
If Joseph is to be a type, he is to be a perfect type Amen. In verse 28: his brothers are beginning to see that God is behind these things. As did Nicodemus in the Gospel of John (3:1-10; 7:50; 19:39-42).

V:36: Jacob believed the lie concerning his son Joseph. The lie being, his son was dead. The Jew's nation as a whole also believes the lie, concerning God's Son. That He wasn't God's Son, Neither did He rise from the Dead. Jacob is about to find out that his beloved son is not dead. As the Jewish nation is also about to find out (Zechariah 12:10, Hosea 5:15, thru chapter 6:1-3; and Isaiah 63:1-6; Zechariah 14:1-5).

CHAPTER 43:

V:1, 2: Remember, Simeon is still bound in Egypt. His brothers have returned to their father Jacob. And here we see Jacob telling his sons to return to Egypt, for they have eaten all the grain that Joseph gave them. Also note their lack of concern for their brother Simeon. The Holy Spirit is allowing us to see the true Character of these men. As it was when they sold Joseph, it still is. But God is about to deal with them by the lack of natural resources. V:11-12: They take double the money and gifts, to try once again to buy the bread of life (grain). But note 44:1, Joseph will not accept their money. V:16: His brothers are to eat in Joseph's house (Revelation 19:7-8). If you look into verses 16-19 carefully you will see that a unnamed servant prepares the meal. In verse 23 this unnamed servant speaks to them, "Be not afraid" (John 6:20; 16:13). Also note that Joseph makes provisions for his brothers while they are in a strange land (Ezekiel 11:16). V:26-27: Note Joseph's concern for his family (John 19:26-27).

CHAPTER 44:1:

This chapter speaks on it's own. What I do see is in V:16-33, where Judah makes intercession for Benjamin. As the Lion of the tribe of Judah also did for us (Genesis 49:9-10; Revelation 5:5-6).

CHAPTER 45:1-

V:1; Joseph reveals himself to his brothers (Zechariah 12:10, 11: Isaiah 63:1-6).
V:3: But he does not reveal himself until the second time in which they appear before Joseph, As it was with Moses, as it was with Joshua, as it is with our Savior Himself. Its not until the second appearing (Romans 11:25, 26; Acts 15:12-16; Hosea 5:15 thru 6:3; Zechariah 12:10, 11; 14:1-5; Isaiah 63:1-6:). In verse 4; Joseph makes mention of their betrayal. As Zechariah speaks of concerning our Lord, in (Zechariah 12:10, 11; and 13:6, and John 1:10, 11). As the Jewish leadership betrayed Jesus in (Matt 12:24; Matt 26:3-4). In verse 5, Joseph knew it was God behind the scene. V:7; To preserve a remnant, see V:8, and Zechariah 13:8. Joseph makes mention to God's will in verse 8, to make him Lord over the goverening body of this planet at that time. And to make

Joseph a father to Pharaoh. Egypt is always typed in the scripture as the world. As our Lord will appear the second time to establish His rule, as Psalms 2:1-12 clearly makes mention to (Colossians 1:15-20).

V:9; Israel is sent for by Joseph. As is the Nation Israel in the last days (Mark 13:27). In verse 10 and 11; Joseph speaks of his provisions for them and his desire for them to be near him. In verse 22; each of them is given new clothing (Revelation 19:7, 8; Zechariah 3:1-4). I am in love with verse 24; because I believe the Holy Spirit is speaking to us, "Not to quarrel along the way". In verse 25-26, his brothers go forth to proclaim his glory. As will we, along with the Jewish Nation (Ephesians 3:6).

GENESIS
CHAPTER 46:1-

V:1; Jacob is refered to as Israel. Also note he is offering sacrifices to God. Also notice whenever Jacob is in the Spirit he is made mention to by the Holy Spirit as Israel. But when Jacob is walking in the flesh, he is refered to as Jacob. And this is also made mention to in relation to the Jewish Nation as a whole (Isaiah 40:27, 41:8, 44:1,). Note please verse 2, the scripture states, "God spoke to Israel and Jacob." Then see the verses mention above, this sets our foundation in relation to the names when they are used by the Holy Spirit. In verse three God makes a promise to Jacob, "FOR I WILL MAKE YOU INTO A GREAT NATION THERE" (see 45:7). Note please this promise to Jacob had its origin in Genesis 15:1-18, where God makes a covenant with Abraham in relation to Abraham's offspring (seed) meaning descendants and the land. (Genesis 17:19; 28:13-15).

God states that He is the God of the round trip. Meaning, what He starts He will finish (Genesis 28:15; Hebrews 12:2; Acts 8:26-40). In verse 28; Judah is sent ahead of Israel to Joseph. As the lion of the trib of Judah is sent ahead of us to prepare rooms for us (Genesis 49:9-10; Revelation 5:5-6; John 14:1-3). As He will also be sent ahead of the Nation Israel to do battle in His second advent (Isaiah 63:1-6; Zechariah 14:1-5 which equals Revelation 19:11-16). Note please, Judah was sent ahead of Israel so Israel might know the way!!! To the best of the Land (45:18). In chp 4 46:21-34; Joseph gives instruction, as we receive instruction through God's Holy Word. And Joseph goes before them all to intercede before the King. V:34d; "Then you will be allowed to enter the land Joseph promise." What a interesting chapter. Amen!!!

CHAPTER 47:1-

V:2; Joseph chose 5 of his brothers to present before the king. (John 15:16). Note; the number 5. Five being the number of Grace (Genesis 17:3-8; 17:15-16). Note please, while

God is blessing Abram and Sarai He establishes a covenant with the both of them. And changes the fifth letter in each of their names. A covenant of Grace!!!!!!!!!!!!!!!!!

In verse 7; we see something wondrously strange. We see a man of the field, who has next to nothing in relation to worldly riches blessing the man who has all things in relation to worldly riches. We see Jacob referring to himself as a pilgrim in verse 9; openly confessing his desire not to be seen as one of the world (Hebrew 11:13-16; 32-40). We see the man of God blessing the man of the world. Now, in V:21; Joseph has reduced the people to servitude. As we are willing servants in Christ (Luke 17:10). But he did not touch the land of the worldly priest. (Why)? Because we see God in the book of Exodus dealing with Pharaoh through the Egyptian priesthood. Bringing judgement upon the Egyptian gods. In V;26, Joseph establishes tithes as law in Egypt (Malachi 3:8-10, Matt 22:21). In verse 31; Jacob is referred to as Israel, note please what he is doing (worshiping). This is what I spoke of in chapter 46:1-2, please refer back to those notes.

CHAPTER 48:1-

Please look at verse 5; Jacob takes unto himself, Joseph's two son born to Joseph in Egypt. Jacob claims them as his. As Reuben and Simeon our his. This is very interesting for a number of reasons. One of them being. When you study the Genealogies of Jacob meaning the 12 sons or the 12 tribs of Israel, one of the sons or tribs may or may not be excluded. But there will always be 12 tribs listed. As in Revelation 7:5-8, Dan is missing, but Manasseh is recorded. And please don't fall into the false teaching that Dan is one of the missing tribes of Israel. Because if we study scripture closely we note in James Epistle chapter 1:1 "To the twelve tribes scattered among the nations" James knew they weren't lost. And please take your Bible and turn with me to Ezekiel 48:1, 5. This is durning the Millennial Reign of Christ Jesus our Lord. Note V;1, Dan is the first to receive land alotment and Ephraim shows up in verse 5 of said chapter. So neither is lost. And this is just two of many such examples, and does not God know all things? So how can any of them be lost.
In V;11; We see the loving kindness of God spoken by Israel (Jacob) (Job 42:12-17).
In v:14; Israel blessed the youngest of Joseph Son's. As he himself was blessed of Isaac (Genesis 27:28-29). Note please verse 15-16; Israel gives all glory to God. But pay close attention to the structure, "GOD, Shepherd, Angel, He" (Zechariah 3:1-4; Judges 13:16-18). Studying verse 19 closely using Hebrews 11:21 as a commentary we are given great insight into the fact that Israel spoke by the Divine Revelation of God as he was being moved, or carried along by the Holy Spirit. Looking back to verse 10, we see that Israel's physical eyes were failing him and he could hardly see. But, with the eyes of his heart, that is spiritually, he was able to see much better then his son Joseph. Because Joseph

wished the blessing to fall upon the firstborn, but Israel refused (V:19). Studying from verse 14, forward unto the end of said chapter, you will see that Israel was speaking by the Holy Spirit. For he spoke of the future of the two boys and that which was yet to take place in Joseph's life.

CHAPTER 49:1-

Chapter 49, is a chapter of great prophecy. The statements of Jacob concerning his sons reach far into the future. Even future of this day. Some are hard to understand some are easy. And to explain them all would take 20 pages in and of itself. Please remember this is a study typing Joseph as a model, pattern, foreshadowing of Jesus. Not a study of chapter 49 in all its fullness. But there are a few points of interest which need to be expounded upon. V:8; "Judah" means praise. The right of the firstborn (Reuben) past on to Joseph's two sons, because of Reuben transgression (Genesis 49:1-4; 1 Chronicles 5:1) Now focusing on V:8, 9, 10, We move into a prophecy revealing that the Messiah would come through the tribe of Judah. In verse 8, we see the future sovereignty of the tribe of Judah.

Which even becomes more focus in verse 9 and verse 10. "YOU ARE A LION'S CUB," O JUDAH; MY SON" (Revelation 5:5) V:9d "WHO DARES TO ROUSE HIM" (Psalm 2:12). V:10; THE SCEPTER WILL NOT DEPART FROM JUDAH, NOR THE RULERS STAFF FROM BETWEEN HIS FEET, UNTIL HE COMES TO WHOM IT BELONGS, This is speaking of the right to rule or inflict justice. This is a prophecy speaking to the fact that the right of the Jewish Nation to rule and govern itself would be taken from them when "Shiloh" came. Which happened about 8AD. But Shiloh had come by 8AD the Christ child was teaching in the temple (Luke 2:41-52). So the prophecy wasn't broken. As the Jews of those days thought. Note V:11; Donkey, colt, (Zechariah 9:9). V:11; "Branch," (Isaiah 11:1, 2=Revelation 5:5). V:11; "He will wash His garments in wine, His robes in the blood of grapes (Isaiah 63:1-6, Revelation 14:18-20). (Revelation 19:11-16 and Zechariah 14:1-5). So in Genesis 49:8-11; God has revealed more of His Divine plan. In relation to His Son. And we see it carry itself all the way into the book of Revelation. Now on to chapter 50.

CHAPTER 50:1-

Verses 1-10; speak in and of themselves. But when we come to V:10, we see the scripture stating "Joseph observed a seven day period of mourning (Job 2:13; Ezekiel 3:15). This seven day period appears to be the norm for mourning. When we reach verse 15 and read through to verse 17, we see Joseph's brothers are still not trusting in God. They are trusting in the foolishness of their own hearts, and the efforts of their flesh. The first thing they do is lie to Joseph. Revealing their poor spiritual state of being. They have yet to learn from their experiences. This should be our prayer, "<u>LORD LET NOT THESE LESSONS BE WASTED</u>." As the LORD asked Adam in Genesis 3:9, "<u>WHERE ART THOU</u>." We should ask of ourselves. (2 Corinthians 13:5). At the end of verse 17, we see Joseph's tears. The Love of his heart, his compassion, and his concern for their needs and their fallen spiritual state. We see the heart of God working in Joseph. As we all know and understand in our own hearts the Love of God found only in Christ Jesus our Lord. In verse 19, Joseph speaks the words "Be not Afraid" as our beloved Savior spoke on a number of occasions (John 20:19e). In verse 20, he speaks of the remnant of God (Zechariah 18:8, Isaiah 27:12-13, 11:10-11). Verse 21, "I will provide for you and your Children" (Exodus 20:6, John 6:5-13). Note, the Book of Genesis starts with life in relation to all things. The Birth of man, and ends in a coffin. With the one who most models or types our Savior. The man Christ Jesus, whom like Joseph would lay in a rich mans tomb (Isaiah 53:9; John 19:38-42). Not for the coffin of Jopseh death of man, but that man might live unto everlasting life.

THE BOOK OF GENESIS IS THE BOOK OF BEGINNINGS<br>THE POWER OF CREATION<br>LIFE FROM LIFELESSNESS

THE BIRTH OF A NATION, NURTURED BY GOD, TO<br>BRING FORTH THE MAN CHRIST JESUS

Please note: Joseph was laid in a coffin, the Hebrew word used here is ARK, how interesting.

Please note: From chapter 41:40 thru the end of chapter 50: Joseph was ruling or governing over the known world at that time. But, even in this position of authority Joseph chose not to contact his brothers. (Why). We see the same thing when we look towards our Savior. Though He has all authority even to this very day, He chooses not to make contact with His brothers as of yet. Not until His second appearing before them, as it was with Joseph (45:3-9) (Hosea 5:15-6:3). Joseph ministered to his brothers through correction. As does our Lord (Revelation 3:19; Job 5:17; Jeremiah 7:28; 1 Corinthians 11:32).

ADDITIONAL SIDE NOTES

Now that we have worked through the typology of Joseph in relation to Christ Jesus from chapter 37, to the closing of chapter 50. I would like to back up to chapter 37; to touch on a very interesting passage of scripture, which at the time of this study would of taken from our major train of thought.

Take your Bibles please and turn with me to Revelation chapter 12.. In Revelation 12:1-6 we see a women clothed with the sun, with the moon under her feet and a crown of twelve stars on her head. This women was pregnant, and was about to give birth to a child. In verse 5, she gives birth to a son, a male child, who will rule all the nations with an iron scepter. And her child was snatched up to God and to His Throne. The women fled into the desert to a place prepared for her by God.

Many teach this women mentioned here is the Church or the bride of Christ. Not so. For one, the church did not give birth to the Christ child. The church was established by the completed work of our Christ. And if this is the bride (church) she is in trouble because she is pregnant. For the bride of Christ is to be as a pure virgin to Him (2 Corinthians 11:2). To present her to Himself as a radiant church, without stain or wrinkle or any other blemish, but Holy and Blameless (Ephesians 5:25-27). The answer to whom this women is will be found in the Word of God when we rightly divide or correctly handly the Word of truth (meaning cross referencing). Turn with me please to Genesis 37:9, 10; where we will see that Jacob himself gives us the answer to this most frequently miss taught passage of scripture. In verse 9 of Genesis 37 Joseph has a second dream. This time the sun, and the moon and eleven stars were bowing down to him. In verse 10 of this passage Jacob gives us the answer to Revelation 12:1-6, by his statement in verse 10. Jacob clearly teaches us that the sun and the moon are Joseph's father and mother. And the eleven stars are Joseph's brothers. But this passage of scripture in Revelation 12:1-6, goes back even further then Jacobs statement in Genesis 37:9, 10. Because the passage in Revelation involves also the prophecy of Genesis 3:15. The promise of God in relation to a deliverer through the seed of the women. The Women is the nation Israel, but strangely enough tracing itself back all the way to Eve and the promise of God in the garden of Eden. Note, after the prophecies in Genesis 3:15-19; Adam changes the name of his wife from women to Eve. Proclaiming her to be the mother of all the living (spiritual living). Others teach the women mentioned here in Revelation 12:1-6; is Mary the mother of Jesus. Not so. Where in the scripture does it teach that Mary the mother of Jesus ever fled into the desert (wilderness) it does not. But, the scripture does teach us that The nation Israel will flee into the desert (wilderness) yet future of this day durning the years of tribulation (or the time of Jacob's trouble, Jeremiah 30:7-Matthew 24:15-16-22). (Daniel 9:27 - 2 Thessalonians 2:3-5). (Daniel 9:27;- Daniel 11:36, 41, note please verse 41, Edom is spared the wrath of the Coming world leader (anti-christ). Why? Answer. Isaiah 63:1-6; note please the remnant of Israel is hiding there. As Revelation states. As the Lord Himself makes mention of in Matthew 24:15-22. Please study Daniel

9;27; then take a look at Daniel 12:11; then jump over to Revelation chapter 12:6; note the days mentioned in all three passages of scripture.

Please note; ACTS 17:11:
Please note; This study in all its fullness is only, meant to be guide as you open the pages of your Bible looking into these matters.

GOD Bless:

# MOSES AND JESUS

Here in these pages are a true comparison of the similitudes or likeness's between Moses in the Old Testament and Jesus the Christ made manifest in the New Testament. Similitudes means being similar to likeness, paralled or a "type" of something else or someone in comparison.

What they have in common to each other.

Though it may seem that Jesus is nowhere to be seen in the Old Testament, by reading these proofs. You may find that Moses was a "type" of Jesus in several ways. Both were sent by the Father God to perform a specific yet mighty task to accomplish - His great work to save the Isralea people on this earth.

Please read on to investigate these facts and you will find that Jesus in "typed," in every event that happened in Moses life.

(The scriptures are taken from The Holy Bible) NIV Study Bible Zondervan. Red Letter Edition 1978

In Deut 18:15-18, Moses speaks of this very one that will be raised up among his bretheren, a prophet.. His Name is Jesus.

They both had endangered lives.

Moses as with Jesus both were Israelites, (Jews) born in a time of Gentile bondage having their very lives endangered by the rulers of their times. Upon fleeing, their lives were saved to fulfill their purpose, Moses - to save the Israelites from God Himself and Pharoh. Jesus - to save the remnant ⅓ (Zec 13:8) & (Acts 15:16-18) of Israel and all of mankind who will call upon the Name of the Lord and be saved, with the promise of eternal life.

## Had Egypt in Common

Moses' life was saved by the daughter of the Pharoh of Egypt, positioning him to be the next in line to the royal throne.

Where Jesus had an earthly mother yet his father was and is still enthroned in the heavenlies, where Jesus will be seated. (Rev 3:21)

Egypt play a significant role in both of their lives.

(Matthew 2:13&14) Jesus

(Exodus 2:1-11) Moses

## Mission to Save

They both had a mission to be Saviors of peoples, being accepted of them, yet being rejected by them. (Exodus 2:11-15) Moses

(Luke 19:28-44 & Matthew 21:1-11) Jesus

Moses and Jesus were Shepherds.

Looked upon as the lowest of professions. Moses was a shephard in Midian for 40 yrs until God told him to return to Egypt to save his fellow bretheren from cruel bondage, (Exodus 3 (all)) Moses which he did.

Jesus is the great shepherd saving not only the Jews, but the gentiles that come to accept him as Savior. Both leading people out of bondage. Jesus being the great shephard, will not only save people, he will restore all things.

## First Miracles

The first miracle thru Moses occured in (Exodus 4:2-4) referring to the rod he had in his hand. Upon God's command, Moses threw down the rod and it became a serpant, then shortly returning back to a rod.

In (Exodus 4:4-6) upon God's command Moses taking his hand out his cloak, normal, then instantly turned leoparous. God then changes it back.

Jesus first miracle is recorded in (John 2:9-11) changing water into wine at a wedding banquet of a gentile bride.

## Washed their brethren with Water

Moses washed Aaron and his sons in water for cleansing in Lev. 8:6, required before ceremonies.

Jesus washing the disciples feet in John 13:4-10

## Reward Gods Servants

Moses rewarding the heads of the tribes, the princes of Israel in Numbers 7:2-5

Jesus bringing his reward to every man according to his work in Rev. 22:12

Building a tabernacle
Moses in Exodus 40:2-38 until it was finished (vs 33)

Jesus as in Zec. 6:12 & 13 where it is stated as "the branch" shall build the temple and bare the glory of it.

## Both had Authority to Anoint

As commanded by God, Moses was given instruction on anointing the tabernacle and the responsible priests for their service in Lev. 8 (all)

Jesus anoints with fire and the Holy Spirit on all waiting for it in Acts 2 (all)

Both Completed their Tasks

Moses had completed all God had told him to do in Lev. 40:32 then also in Deut 34:1-12

Jesus also finishing the work he was sent to do in John 17:4 spoken by Jesus himself and John 19:30, Jesus stating that "It is finished."

Both died to benefit Gods People

Moses, knowing he would not make it to the promised land seeks to make sure, Israel moves forward, read Deut 3:26-29 & Deut 33 (all) & 34 (all)

Jesus, yeilding up the ghost with aloud cry in Matt 27:50-53 and mighty things happened there at his death, dying once, for all, a blood sacrafice that will be forever unmatched in the history of Man and Creation.

Both had appointed others to
<u>follow after them to carry on.</u>

Moses had Joshua (Deut 33:9) to carry on forward to enter the Promised Land.

Jesus, "the Sent One," died leaving the great commission, please read 1 John 5 (all) to understand to become children of God are all those that believe on Jesus the Christ. Promising the sending of the Holy Spirit before His ascension and Eternal life in (vs 11). Notice the word "whosoever" in verse 1 of chapter 5. That means anyone that will call upon the Lord, even today. The death of Jesus wasn't the end it was the beginning of the veil being rent and "we", me & you can enter in, thru prayer and praise and glory to praise the unmatched Majesty of Jesus Our Lord!!

## Summary

Throughout the lives of Moses and Jesus, their divine appointment was fulfilled. Though they had obstacles to get past and difficult tasks to perform, they were done by Gods Mighty Power. Though their lives were endangered, God intervened to ensure that their tasks were performed to the end. Though they were meek and seemed lowly, they were made strong by the power of God Almighty to perform some of the greatest tasks on this earth known to mankind untill this day, with much greater events to come. (Rev 4:1) forward.

I hope you may see that reading the Old Testament is important for understanding that the very people Moses saved from the bondage of Egypt, lead through the desert, to God's Promised Land are the same people that will be dealt with by Christ our Lord in the end of the New Testament bringing the remnant with him to dwell in The New Jerusalem. Let these writings inspire you to seek all of God's word throughout the Holy Bible. Many blessings upon you today and always.

# REVELATION OVERVIEW

Inside these few pages contain many but brief facts

Found in the book of Revelation. Revelation, seeming to be
the most complexing and difficult book to understand,
does indeed bring resolve and conclusion to all that came
before it! A complete unveiling of what the Holy Bible

Calls, "The Little Apocalypse"

Here is the total redemption of all things made by Christ.

In Genesis, sin originated, in Revelation it is abolished.

Please read this overview and see that it is a sketch of a
bigger picture in a simpler form, yet realize that the time

Is now at hand, facing us today and the near future.

REV. 1:19

# REVELATION OVERVIEW

The title of the book and the opening word of the book in chapter one vrs. 1: Revelation - The English transliteration of the Greek word Apocalypse; "Strong's reference" 602; Apokalupsis (ap-ok-al-oop-sis); Disclosure: - Appearing, Coming, Lighten, Manifestation, Be Revealed (Revelation). Prime root 601. To take off the covers, ie. disclose, reveal, make known, unveiling. Scriptural references: Amos 3:7, 4:13; Gen. 40:8, 41:16; Daniel 2:28, 9:22-23; John 15:15, 16:7-15, 17:3-6; Rev. 1:1, 1:19.

The Book of Revelation was written about the time of 54 AD to 95 AD. One of the main keys to understanding the book is found in the title itself. The writings are to be understood. Note: chapter 1 vrs. 19, three commands are given to structure or pattern the writings (book).

1st command; write what you have seen, chapter one.

2nd command; what is now, Church Age = chapters 2 & 3. The seven dictated Letters to the Churches.

3rd command; and what will take place after these things: chapter 4:1 through the closing of the book; After the Church Age.

There are 404 verses contained within the writings of this book in which 357 of them are direct quotes from the Old Testament, 800 references to the entire Bible itself. So we are led by the Holy Spirit to perceive the writings as a complex coded message system. The result will force us to familiarize ourselves with the entire Bible and depend upon God's unveiling of this coded message through the understanding of scripture; 2nd Tim. 2:15; Prov. 25:2 = Isa. 28:9-10 (refer to the King James version).

The Book of Revelation is the completed unveiling of the other 65 books of the Bible. Such manifestations are seen in what some scholars call this collection "The Little Apocalypse". Isaiah chapter 24 through 27 portrays this and such statements as "My Spirit will not contend with man forever, for he is mortal" Gen. 6:3, Isa. 34:1-8, 63:1-6, 65:17, 66:15-16, 22; Joel 3:1-3; Zech. 14:1-5; Matt. 24:21-31; Heb. 1:10-12, 1:10, 13-16; 2nd Peter 3:5-13; Jude vrs. 14-16; and many more such passages. These all point ahead to the coming apocalypse; The Revelation.

The Book has great structure hidden within the text. Remember, it is completely orchestrated by God, the master of communication. In Ist Chr. 24:7-18 we see that King David divided the priesthood into 24 courses. In the Book of Exodus, Aaron and his sons are mentioned 24 times and they were the Priesthood. In Revelation there are 24 titles given to Jesus, such as: 1:2 Jesus Christ", vrs. 5 "Faithful Witness", "Firstborn",

"Ruler of the Kings", Vrs. 8 "The Alpha & Omega", "Lord God", "Almighty", 1:13 "Son of Man", vrs. 17 "First and Last", 2:18 "Son of God", 3:7 "Holy & True", 3:14 "Amen" (Isa. 65:16 & 2 Cor. 1:20), 5:6 "Thy Lamb", 19:13 "The Word", 19:16 "King of Kings and Lord of Lords", and so on... Also, note in chapter 4:4 24 thrones with 24 elders sitting upon them. They are also Priests; 1:6 - 5:10 = 1st Pet. 2:5, 9. Though there are many title (names) given to or of The Lord in chapters 1-3.

Now that we have mentioned the number 7, lets move on to observe the many sequences of 7 in the book we are studying.

The sequences of 7's are mentioned 52 times that I am aware of; 1:4 = seven spirits; 1:11 = seven churches. Some scholars see the number 7 through out scripture as a declaration of "perfection" while others interpret this number to signify both perfection and "completeness". With this in mind, lets move on..

There are 52 sequences of sevens mentioned in Revelation (that I am aware of). Note the following:

| | |
|---|---|
| 1:4 | seven spirits |
| 1:11 | seven churches |
| 1:12 | seven golden lampstands |
| 1:16 | seven stars |
| 1:20 | seven stars, seven lampstands in chapters 2 & 3 plus the seven letters to the seven churches (already mentioned). |

Note also:

| | |
|---|---|
| 4:5 | seven lamps, seven spirits |
| 5:1 | a scroll with seven seals. |
| 5:5 | seven seals and the seven seals of 6:1 |
| 7:12 | seven proclamations are made: praise, glory, wisdom, thanks, honor, power, and strength. |
| 8:1 | the seventh seal |
| 10:4 | "seal up what the seven thunders have said" |
| 11:13 | seven thousand people are killed |
| 11:15 | the seventh angel |
| 13:2 | seven heads |
| 15:1 | seven angels and seven plaques |
| 16:1 | seven angels and seven bowls |
| 16:17 | seventh angel poured out his bowl into the air; "Question" Why the air? See Eph. 2:2, 6:10-12, Rev. 17:1, 3, 10, and v.19. |

In chapter 18:22-24 seven things are mentioned and these are just a few which I chose to mention here. "Question" Is it possible that God is trying to communicate to us through the constant use of the number "7". It would certainly appear so... (review Matt. 5:17-18).

In Revelation 21:1, there are 3 divisions mentioned:
(1)  New Heavens
(2)  New Earth
(3)  No more sea
Interesting, in Exodus 20:11 there we see this division of three men-in two different ways.

In Genesis, we have the beginning of man's arts, religion, and science in rebellion, or separation from God. This is seen or established mainly in Adam's fall, The flood of Noah, and Nimrod and the Tower of Babel (Gen. 10:8 - 11:9). We see, of coarse, the full glory of this established religious and governmental rebellion judged and destroyed in mystery Babylon of Revelation (chapters 17 & 18).

In Genesis, we see a flood by the hand of God destroying an evil generation. In Revelation, we have a flood by Satan to try and destroy God's elect (Rev. 12:15). Genesis has Sodom and Egypt, as does Revelation (in a spiritual sense seen in 11:8 and chapters 17 & 18).

In Genesis, we have a plot against Abraham by Satan which is overthrown by God (Gen. 12:10-20, 20:1-7). In Revelation, the attack is against Abraham's seed, God's Son, and descendants as found in Rev. 12:11-17.

In Genesis we have the marriage of the first man Adam, in Revelation we have the marriage of the second man Adam (1st Cor. 15:45; Rev. 19:7-9). In Genesis, we have a bride for Abraham's son, in Revelation, a bride for God's Son. The Promise of Genesis 22:17-18 is to Abraham and his seed; "They shall take possession of the cities of their enemies". The promised seed, of coarse, does take possession of all things promised before the closing of this book.

In Genesis, man's dominion ceased and Satan's dominion of the earth began. In Revelation, Satan's dominion is ended and man's dominion is restored in Christ.

The whole concept of Gen. 3:15 "The seed of the woman" is, of coarse, exactly what Rev. 12:1-6 is all about. The whole idea of the seed of the woman, the Virgin Birth, and the Seed of a Kinsman is seen in Gen. 3:15, the Book of Ruth, Rev 5:1-6 and 12:1-6.

The idea of coats of skin (Gen. 3:21), the covering of blood, or the offering of 4:4 of Genesis, and the way to the Tree of Life which is blocked in Gen. 3:23-24, is freely accessible in Revelation.

The role of the serpent in Genesis 3:1-15, is seen more clearly in Rev. 12:1 thru and his final fate is clearly portrayed in Rev. 20:1-3, 7-10. In the Old Testament, Exodus is the Book of redemption. In the New Testament, the book of Revelation manifests the consummation of this redemption.

The issue in the Book of Revelation is not so much one of salvation, but redemption and restoration. Note: I didn't divorce this from salvation, but, the main thrust of the script is redemption and restoration of all things (restoring that which was lost in Genesis). This isn't just man, there is a New Heavens and a New Earth in v 21:1 and Romans 8:19-24.

Revelation 21:21, the 12 gates of the New Jerusalem, are 12 Pearls. The Lord teaches us in Matt. 13:45 of the Kingdom being as a Pearl (Interesting). Why? A pearl is a Gentile gem stone because it comes from a shell fish which is unclean to a Israelite (Lev. 11:9-10; Dt. 14:9-10). The pearl is the only gem stone produced by a living organizum. Given life and growth through earritation, it grows in the sea. Then it is removed from it's place of growth. It then becomes an item of adornment: (Mal. 3:16 & 17). Facinating!

I hope and pray this overview will help us approach God's word in a different light. Possibly it may blindfold some of our own prejudices and allow the Holy Spirit to lead us through the scriptures without us throwing up so many walls before His guidance. I pray this short summary will inspire us to look even deeper into God's Word.

REMEMBER: Acts 17:11 always applies..

As written By Moses in Genesis 5.

Below is written the names in the bloodline from Adam to Noah. Each name having a meaning together, speaks of Gods redemptive plan describing His Son Jesus.

| Hebrew | = | English |
|--------|---|---------|
| Adam | | Man |
| Seth | | Appointed |
| Enoch | | Mortal |
| Kenan | | Sorrow |
| Mahalaleel | | The blessed God |
| Jared | | Shall come down |
| Enoch | | Teaching |
| Methuselah | | His death shall bring |
| Lamech | | the disparing |
| Noah | | rest or comfort |

The mission of Jesus, which will be completed in the book of Revelation.

# BODILY RESURRECTION

These two sections of the book on Bodily Resurrection and (Pre Daniel 9:27) rapture are good study guides in a small group setting to help fellow believers to understand in depth that God will save those that belong to him from the coming wrath of tribulation that is to come in the last days. The promise of the ressurrected, glorified body is ours also at this time.

Please search out these scriptures and see that we have a glorious hope in Jesus' return weither we be awake and alive or asleep in our grave waiting for the call.

Thank Him that he spares those that belong to him from this destruction. Amen.

## A Bodily Ressurection

The scriptures speak of many diverse passages about the glorified body of Christ and what we will become as those that belong to Him. Please read these passages below to verify what we are awaiting.

Matthew 28:1-10

Mark 16:6-14

Hosea 13:14

Luke 24:5-44

John 20:all

Acts 1:9-11

Rev 1:13-18

Rev 5:6

Phillipians 3:20-21

1 John 3:2-3

II Kings 2:9-13

Matthew 27:50-53

Romans 8:17-23

Job 19:25-27

John 11:25-26

John 11:39-43

Isiah 26:19, 20

Matthew 17:1-2

1 Cor 15:35-57

Job 14:13-14

Genesis 5:24

Daniel 12:1-3

## Pre Daniel 9:27 - Caught-up Raptured

Below are scriptures that will verify that the "believer" in Christ will be removed, caught-up, taken out of the way, raptured. Please search out these scriptures and know that in this present day, believers around the world are anxiously awaiting this event to take place, saving us from tribulation.

I Thessalonians 4:13-18

I Cor 15:50-57

Luke 21:34-36

Romans 5:9-11

I Thess. 1:10, 5:9

II Peter 4-7

Rev 3:10

John 14:1-4

Isiah 26:20-21

Zeph 2:2-3

Romans 11:25-26

Acts 15:14-18

II Thess 2:3-10

Isiah 57:1

Psalm 27:5

Genesis 5:24

Hebrews 13:8

Genesis 19:22

Gen 18:20-33

Luke 21:18-24

Joel 2:16

Rev. 4:1-2 &

Rev. 5:9

Daniel 3:17

Genesis 7:1-5

Matthew 16:18

# OUR COMING KING

While studying under Chuck Missler's ministry at

Calvary Chapel, Costa Mesa, Calif. He was teaching on the different attributes that state what and who Jesus is and that He is coming in all His glory to take his bride!!

I was amazed at Chucks collection of titles and descriptions that I approached Mr. Missler after service about using this information to reach the lost for Christ. Chuck responded that it is God's word and that I could use Our Coming King in any fashion I saw fit for ministry.

So, on that note. Here it is!!

This will give you a broader picture for understanding Who Christ is if you don't know him and a better understanding of Him if you do!!

OUR COMING KING

The lion of the Tribe of Judah
He is a Racial King
He is the King of the Jew's
He is a National King
He will rule the known world through
Isreal sitting on his throne
in Isreal
He is our Messiah, our Christ, our
Deliverer, our Husband
Though is is Jewish...

We are His Church, His Bride
founded and established by Jewish
leadership.
Using a collection of books bound
together which we call the Bible
Which is also Jewish

He is the Lord of Lord's
and the King of Kings
He is the King of Glory,
He is the King of Heaven and of
earth...
and he is the King of all the ages...
and my question tonight to all of us is:
Do we know him....do we really know
him?

He is a prophet before Moses
A Priest in the order of Melchizedek
A Champion like Joshua
He is the Offering in the Place of Isaac.

A king from the line of David
A wise Counselor above Soloman

Beloved, though rejecected,
and exalted son like Joseph

The Heavens declare his glory
The firment show His handywork

He who is, who was, and always shall
be, The Lord.

He is the First and the Last
The Beginning and the End
The Alph and Talph
The Alpha and Omaga
The A to Z in our alphabet.

He is the First Fruits of those who sleep...
He is the I Am The I Am...the Great I Am.

He is the Voice of the Buring Bush
He is the Captain of the Lord's Host.
Indearly strong
Entirely sincere
Eternally steadfast
He is Forever Graceful
Impartially Merciful
Emencely Powerful
He is the Concourer of Jerico

In him dwells the fullness of the God
Head bodily

He is our Kingsman Redemer
Our Goal
Our Avenger of Blood
and He is our City of Refuge
and our Ladder as He was Jacob's.

He is our Performing High Priest
Our Personal Prophet
Our Reigning King

He is the Way, the Truth, and the Life
and no one comes to the Father but by Him·

He is the Highest Personality in literature
He is the Supreme Problem
In higher criticisium
He is the Miracle of the Ages
and he is that which make everything good.

You and I are the benificiaries of a
love letter which was
written in blood on a wooden cross
over 2,000 years ago in Jedea.

They say he was crucified on a cross
of wood, though he made the hill on
which it stood.

By him was all things made that was made
and by Him are all things held together.

He was borned of a woman so that
you and I could be borned again,
borned of God.

He humbled himself so that you and I
could be lifted up.

He became a servent so that you and
I could become Joint Heirs with Him.

He suffered rejection so we could
become his
Friends.

He denied himself so we could freely
receive all things.

He gave all of himself so he could
bless us in every way.

He's available, tempted, tried and
found true.

He blesses the young,
cleanses the leopard,
defends the feable.
He heal's the sick
Delivers the captives,
discharges the debtor,
rewards the diligent.
Forgives the sinners,
provides strength to the meek.
Heals the broken hearted,
guards the elderly,
serves the misfortunate,
sympathizes, and He saves.

His love never changes
nor will it ever end.
He is the God of Redemption,
The God of Restoration,
and the Giver of Life.

His offices are manifold,
His reign is rightious
His promises are sure
His goodness is endless,
His light is matchless,
His grace is sufficient,
His mercy is everlasting
          AND
His word is enough!!!!

His yoke is easy,
and his burden is light...

I wish I could describe Him to you.
He is indescrible
He is incomprehenceable

He is irresistible
and, of course, He is invincible

The heaven's can't contain him and
man can't explain him.
The Pharisees can't stand him,
but soon learned they couldn't stop him.

Pilot, The Personal Representitive of
the known world
couldn't find fault with him,
and the witnesses couldn't agree
against him.
Herrod couldn't kill him,
Death couldn't keep him,
The grave couldn't hold him,
He has always been and forever shall be.
He is eternal....future
and he is eternal......past.

He had no predecessor
and he will have no successor.

You cannot impeach him
and He is not going to resign

His name is above every name
and at the name of Jesus every knee shall bow,
Every tongue will confess that Jesus
Christ is Lord.
The Power and the Glory....forever
and ever.
                    AMEN!

He is the Lamb of God which taketh
away the sins of the world,
He is the Ashes of the Red Heifer,
The water of cleansing,
The water of life,

He is the True Bread of Life which
commeth down from heaven.
He is the light of the world.
In him is life and that life is the light of every man.

For God so loved the world he gave
us his son*!!!*

                So be

it.....

                  **AMEN**

# WE ARE LIVING IN NOW.

1. <u>Luke 21:24</u> - Until the full number of the gentiles come in.
2. <u>Luke 21:23-32</u> - ...this generation will not pass away until they see all these things come to pass.
3. <u>2 Thes. 2:7-8</u> - ...but the one that now holds it back will continue to do so until he is taken out of the way.
4. <u>I Timothy 6:14</u> - ...to keep this command without spot or blame until the appearing of our Lord Jesus Christ.
5. <u>II Thes 2:3</u> - ... for that day will not come until...the man of lawlessness is revealed, the man doomed to destruction.
6. <u>Matthew 28:20</u> - The great commission. And surely I am with you always, even until the end of the age.
7. Can you find #7?

Printed in the United States
By Bookmasters